RENAL COOKBOOK

Samuel Hartwell

TEXT COPYRIGHT © Samuel Hartwell

All rights reserved. No part of this guide may be reproduced in any form without permission in writing from the publisher except in the case of brief quotations embodied in critical articles or reviews.

LEGAL & DISCLAIMER

The information contained in this book and its contents is not designed to replace or take the place of any form of medical or professional advice; and is not meant to replace the need for independent medical, financial, legal, or other professional advice or services, as may be required. The content and information in this book has been provided for educational and entertainment purposes only.

The content and information contained in this book has been compiled from sources deemed reliable, and it is accurate to the best of the Author's knowledge, information, and belief. However, the Author cannot guarantee its accuracy and validity and cannot be held liable for any errors and/or omissions. Further, changes are periodically made to this book as and when needed. Where appropriate and/or necessary, you must consult a professional (including but not limited to your doctor, attorney, financial advisor, or such other professional advisor) before using any of the suggested remedies, techniques, or information in this book.

Upon using the contents and information contained in this book, you agree to hold harmless the Author from and against any damages, costs, and expenses, including any legal fees potentially resulting from the application of any of the information provided by this book. This disclaimer applies to any loss, damages or injury caused by the use and application, whether directly or indirectly, of any advice or information presented, whether for breach of contract, tort, negligence, personal injury, criminal intent, or under any other cause of action. You agree to accept all risks of using the information presented inside this book.

You agree that by continuing to read this book, where appropriate and/or necessary, you shall consult a professional (including but not limited to your doctor, attorney, or financial advisor or such other advisor as needed) before using any of the suggested remedies, techniques, or information in this book.

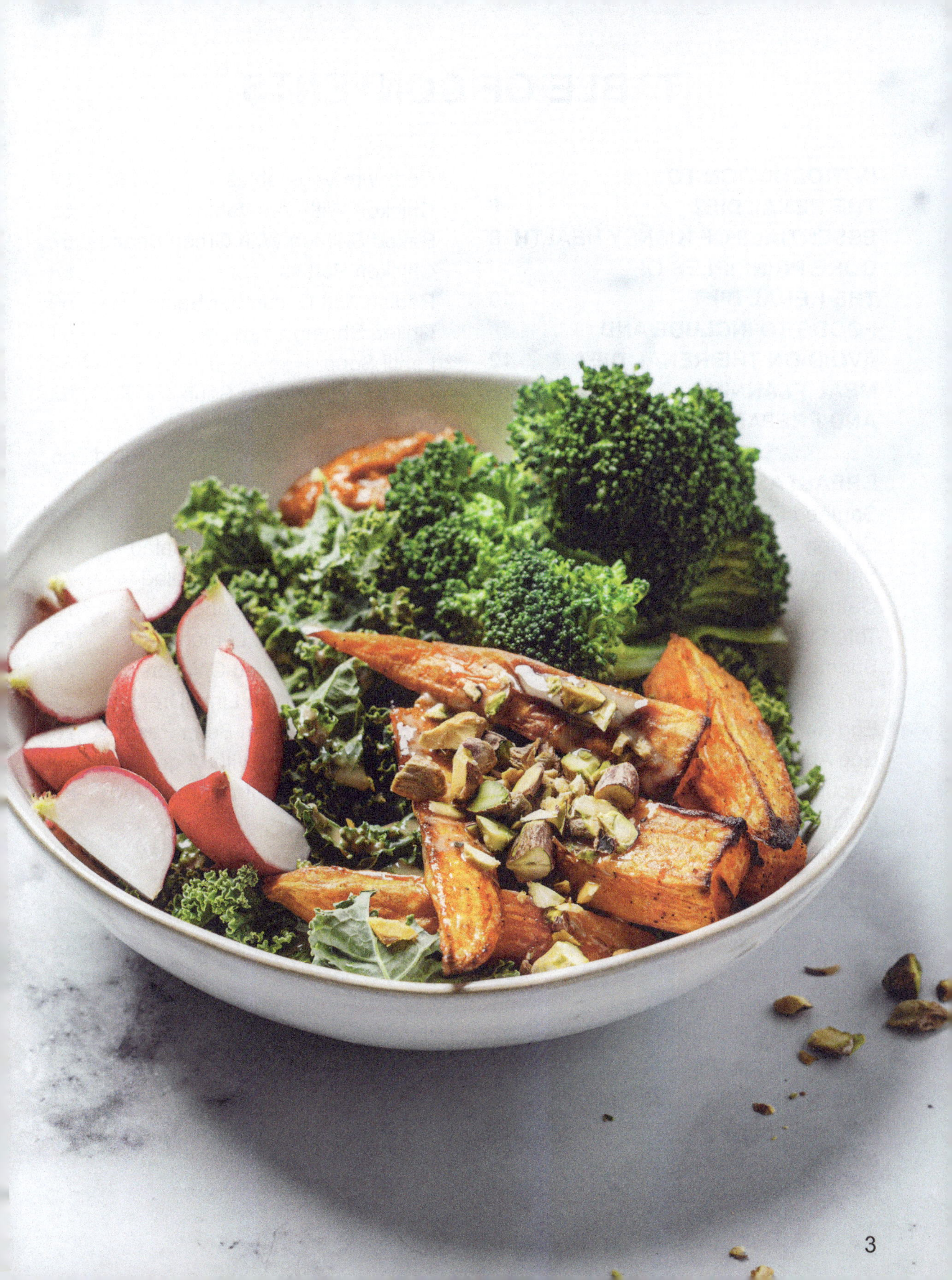

TABLE OF CONTENTS

INTRODUCTION TO THE RENAL DIET 6
ESSENTIALS OF KIDNEY HEALTH 8
CORE PRINCIPLES OF THE RENAL DIET 10
FOODS TO INCLUDE AND AVOID ON THE RENAL DIET 12
MEAL PLANNING AND PREPARATION 16

BREAKFAST RECIPES 20
Sautéed Cabbage With Fried Egg 23
Quinoa Breakfast Bowl 24
Salmon Muffins 25
Oatmeal With Berries 27
Tofu Scramble Toast 29
Shrimp And Eggs Mix 30
Turmeric Scramble 31
Egg And Vegetable Wrap 33
Egg And Salmon Scramble 35
Cucumber, Radish, And Egg Salad 36
Cucumber And Berry Smoothie 37
Blueberry Pancakes 39

MAIN DISH 40
Baked Salmon With Tzatziki Sauce 43
Veggie Roast 44
Fish With Vegetables 45
Lemon Herb Baked Chicken 47
Baked Salmon With Lemon And Herbs 49
Zucchini Fritters 50
Salmon With Broccoli 51
Roasted Turkey Breast 53
Cod With Vegetables 54
Chicken With Vegetables 55
Baked Salmon With Green Beans 57
Chicken Patties 58
Radish And Cucumber Salad 59
Grilled Shrimp Skewers 61
Lentil Soup 62
Creamy Cauliflower Soup 63
Turkey Meatballs With Mint 65
Zucchini And Carrot Ribbon Salad 66
Cabbage And Cucumber Salad 67
Baked Chicken Legs 69
Shrimp And Green Bean Salad 70
Arugula And Cucumber Salad 71
Zucchini Shrimp Spaghetti 73
Green Beans With Lemon-Herb 74
Lemon Garlic Grilled Chicken 75
Salmon Salad With Lime Dressing 77
Zucchini And Green Bean Pasta 78
Chicken Skewers With Vegetables 79
Chicken Thighs With Herbs 81

MAIN DISH 82
Cauliflower Popcorn 85
Renal-Friendly Panna Cotta 87
Strawberry Smoothie 88
Berry Smoothie 89
Asparagus Spears 91
Cauliflower Spread 92
Zucchini Herb Spread 93
Roasted Broccoli Florets 95

CONCLUSION 96

5

Introduction to the Renal Diet

Taking care of kidney health is a crucial part of maintaining overall well-being. The kidneys play a vital role in filtering the blood, removing toxins, balancing fluids and electrolytes, and regulating blood pressure. However, for people with kidney disorders or diseases like chronic kidney disease (CKD), a standard diet may be unsafe or even harmful. This is where the renal diet becomes essential.

The renal diet is a specially designed nutritional plan aimed at reducing the workload on the kidneys, maintaining their function, and slowing the progression of kidney disease. Unlike many popular diets, the renal diet is not intended for weight loss or muscle building. Its primary goal is to minimize the intake of substances that the kidneys struggle to process and to maintain a balance of essential nutrients.

Why is the Renal Diet Important?

The renal diet helps individuals with kidney disease control levels of key electrolytes, such as sodium, potassium, and phosphorus, and manage protein intake. In kidney disease, the ability of the kidneys to filter and remove these substances is reduced, and an excess of them can lead to serious complications, including swelling, high blood pressure, and heart problems.

Key Benefits of the Renal Diet:

Reduces Kidney Workload — Limiting sodium, potassium, and phosphorus helps lessen the strain on the kidneys.

Supports Electrolyte Balance — The diet promotes optimal levels of electrolytes essential for good health.

Manages Protein Intake — Balancing protein intake prevents both deficiency and excess, helping to minimize stress on the kidneys.

Who Should Follow This Diet?

The renal diet is primarily recommended for people with chronic kidney disease and for patients undergoing dialysis or preparing for a kidney transplant. However, it may also benefit those at high risk of kidney disease, including individuals with diabetes, high blood pressure, or cardiovascular conditions.

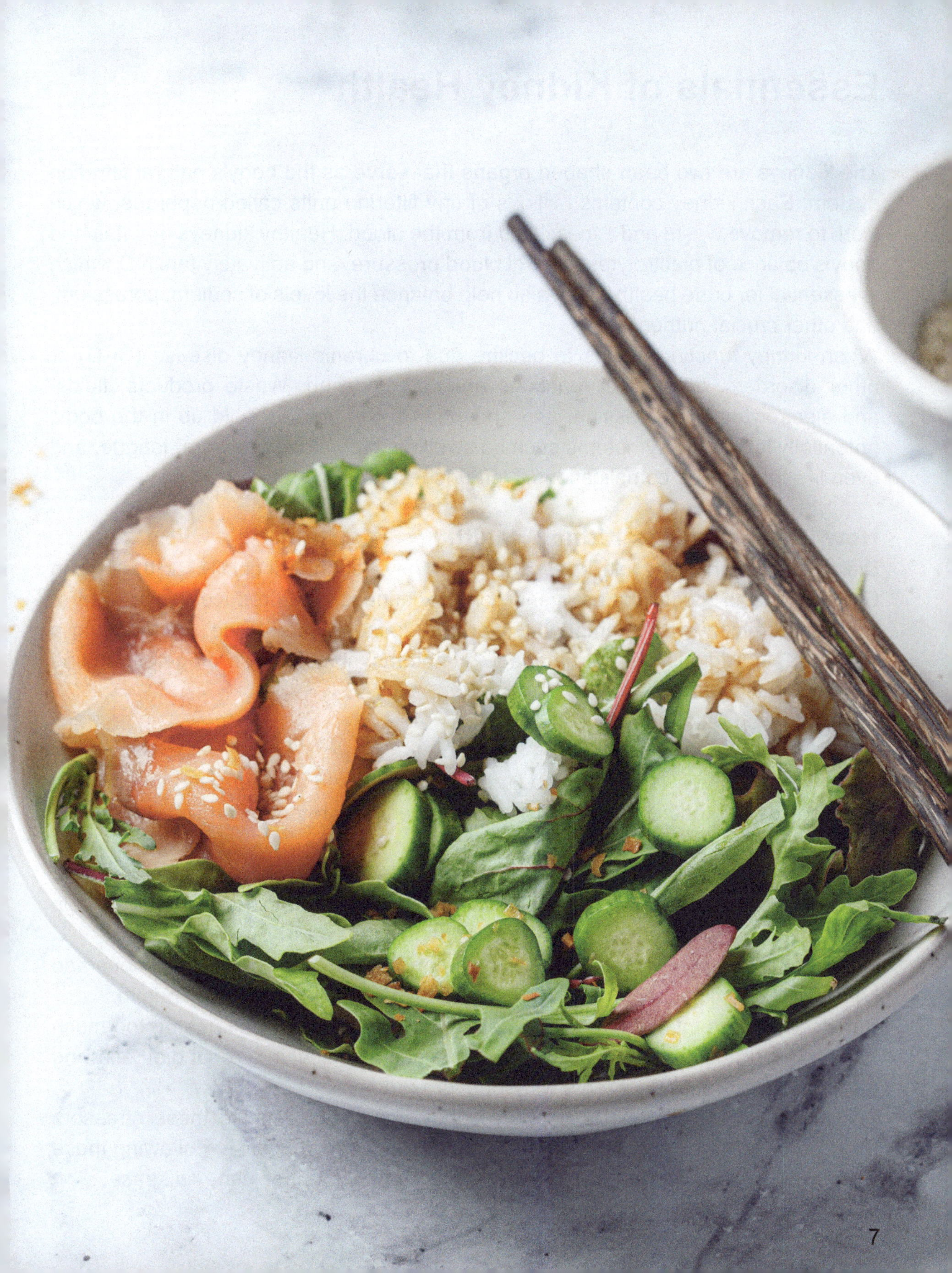

Essentials of Kidney Health

The kidneys are two bean-shaped organs that serve as the body's natural filtration system. Each kidney contains millions of tiny filtering units called nephrons, which work to remove waste and excess fluid from the blood. Healthy kidneys maintain the body's balance of electrolytes, control blood pressure, and activate vitamin D, which is essential for bone health. They also help balance the levels of sodium, potassium, and other crucial nutrients.

When kidney function begins to decline due to chronic kidney disease (CKD) or other disorders, these vital functions are compromised. Waste products, fluids, and electrolytes like potassium and phosphorus can start to build up in the body, potentially leading to symptoms such as swelling, high blood pressure, fatigue, and even life-threatening complications if left unchecked.

How Diet Influences Kidney Health

Diet plays a significant role in supporting kidney health, especially for those with CKD. Choosing foods that are gentle on the kidneys helps reduce the buildup of waste and minimizes the amount of work the kidneys need to do. By following a renal diet, individuals can help manage symptoms, slow disease progression, and improve quality of life.

A well-planned renal diet focuses on:

Sodium Reduction — Too much sodium increases blood pressure and can worsen kidney disease. Reducing salt intake helps prevent fluid retention and reduces strain on the kidneys.

Potassium Control — High potassium levels can be dangerous, especially for people with advanced kidney disease. By choosing low-potassium foods, people can help avoid complications such as irregular heartbeats.

Phosphorus Management — Excess phosphorus in the blood can lead to bone and heart issues. Limiting foods high in phosphorus is essential for kidney health.

Balanced Protein Intake — While protein is necessary for overall health, too much can burden the kidneys. Balancing protein intake is critical in a renal diet, allowing the kidneys to process nutrients without overexertion.

The renal diet is designed to support kidney health by reducing these stressors and making it easier for the kidneys to perform their vital functions. Following these dietary guidelines can significantly impact the management of kidney disease.

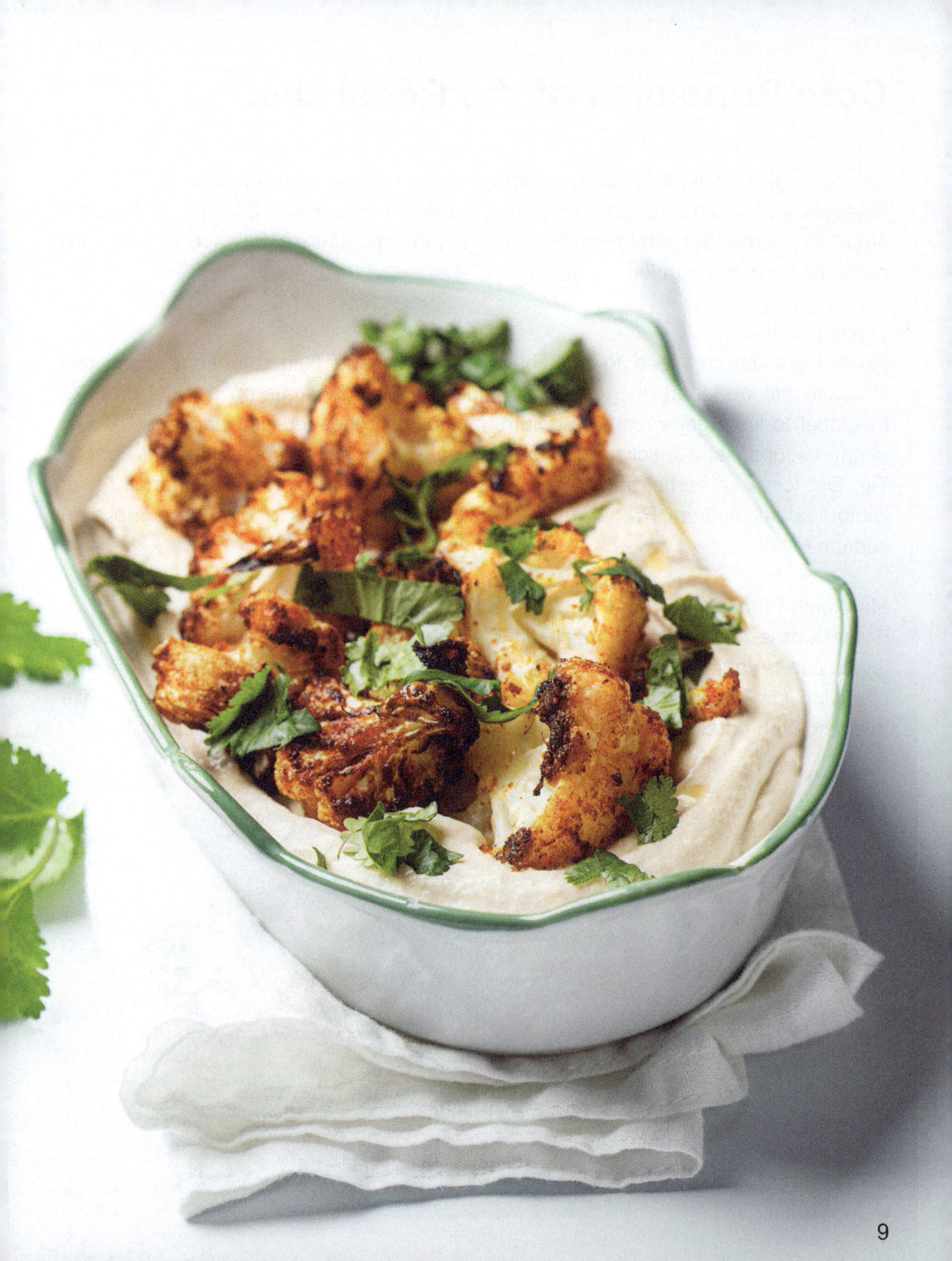

Core Principles of the Renal Diet

The renal diet is tailored to protect kidney health by managing the intake of specific nutrients that could otherwise overburden the kidneys. Each principle of this diet helps to reduce the strain on the kidneys and maintain a balance of essential nutrients for those with kidney disease.

Limiting Sodium
Excess sodium can lead to high blood pressure and fluid retention, which can increase the workload on weakened kidneys. For individuals on a renal diet, it's essential to limit foods high in sodium, including processed and packaged foods, canned soups, salty snacks, and condiments like soy sauce and salad dressings.
Tip: Opt for fresh herbs, spices, and salt-free seasoning blends to enhance flavor without adding sodium. Preparing meals at home also allows for greater control over sodium levels.

Managing Potassium
Potassium is essential for muscle function and heart health, but high potassium levels can be dangerous for those with kidney disease. The renal diet focuses on choosing low-potassium foods, such as apples, berries, and green beans, while avoiding high-potassium options like bananas, oranges, potatoes, and tomatoes.

Tip: Soaking certain vegetables before cooking can help reduce potassium levels. For instance, soaking potatoes and then boiling them can decrease their potassium content.

Controlling Phosphorus
Phosphorus is a mineral that supports bone health, but an excess can lead to weakened bones and cardiovascular issues. Foods such as dairy products, nuts, beans, and certain sodas are often high in phosphorus. To protect kidney health, it's advisable to limit these items or choose low-phosphorus alternatives.
Tip: Check food labels, as many processed foods and beverages contain added phosphorus. Opt for fresh, unprocessed foods whenever possible.

Balancing Protein Intake
Protein is crucial for muscle maintenance and immune health, but an excessive amount can create more waste for the kidneys to process. On a renal diet, protein intake should be balanced to provide enough for bodily functions without overloading the kidneys. Lean proteins like fish, poultry, and egg whites are often good choices, while red meat and processed meats should be limited.
Tip: Work with a healthcare provider or dietitian to determine your ideal protein intake based on the stage of kidney disease. This ensures that you're getting the right amount without straining your kidneys.

Foods to Include and Avoid on the Renal Diet

A renal diet involves carefully choosing foods that support kidney function while minimizing the intake of substances that can overload the kidneys. Below is a guide to the foods you can enjoy and those you should avoid to maintain kidney health.

Foods You Can Enjoy

Low-Potassium Fruits
Fruits are an excellent source of vitamins and antioxidants, but it's essential to choose those that are lower in potassium to protect kidney health. Some of the best options include:
- Apples (fresh, unsweetened)
- Pineapple
- Berries (strawberries, blueberries, raspberries)
- Peaches (fresh or canned, without added sugar)
- Plums

These fruits are nutrient-dense and have a relatively low potassium content compared to high-potassium fruits like bananas and oranges.

Low-Potassium Vegetables
Vegetables are an important source of fiber, vitamins, and minerals. Many vegetables are naturally low in potassium, making them a great choice for the renal diet. Include the following in your meals:
- Green beans
- Cauliflower
- Cucumber
- Zucchini
- Bell peppers
- Carrots (in moderation)

Cooking or soaking some vegetables (such as potatoes or beans) before preparation can reduce their potassium content, making them safer for individuals with kidney disease.

Lean Proteins

Proteins are essential for maintaining muscle mass and overall health, but too much protein can stress the kidneys. Opt for lean sources of protein to meet your nutritional needs without overloading your kidneys. Good choices include:
- Chicken (skinless, baked or grilled)
- Fish (salmon, trout, cod, haddock)
- Egg whites (low in phosphorus compared to whole eggs)
- Tofu (in moderation)

These protein options are typically lower in phosphorus than other animal-based protein sources.

Whole Grains

Whole grains are a great source of fiber and can support digestive health. While it's important to monitor the amount of phosphorus in grains, there are still several kidney-friendly options. Good choices include:
- White rice (lower in potassium and phosphorus compared to brown rice)
- Pasta
- Bread (white or whole-wheat varieties)
- Oats (in moderation)

Be sure to keep portions in check to avoid excessive calorie intake, and pair grains with lean protein and low-potassium vegetables for a well-balanced meal.

Healthy Fats

Healthy fats are important for maintaining heart health, which is critical for individuals with kidney disease. Include these sources of healthy fats in your diet:
- Olive oil
- Avocados (in moderation)
- Nuts and seeds (in small portions)

These fats are heart-healthy and provide essential fatty acids without adding excessive sodium or phosphorus.

It's important to remember that when choosing foods for a renal diet, you should consider your individual health needs, including any allergies or chronic conditions. Always consult with a doctor or dietitian to tailor your diet to your specific situation and ensure it supports kidney health.

Foods to Limit or Avoid

High-Potassium Fruits
Certain fruits are very high in potassium and should be limited or avoided on the renal diet to prevent dangerously high potassium levels, which can lead to heart arrhythmias. These include:
- Bananas
- Oranges
- Tomatoes (fresh or as a sauce)
- Kiwi
- Cantaloupe
- Avocados (in large quantities)

If you enjoy these fruits, it's important to limit their intake and choose lower-potassium options instead.

High-Potassium Vegetables
Like fruits, certain vegetables are also high in potassium. Some of the highest-potassium vegetables include:
- Potatoes (especially sweet potatoes)
- Spinach
- Tomatoes
- Mushrooms
- Beets

For those on a renal diet, it's best to avoid or severely limit these vegetables. However, soaking potatoes and cooking them in water can help reduce potassium content.

High-Phosphorus Foods
Excess phosphorus can harm the bones and heart, and is often found in high quantities in foods such as:
- Dairy products (milk, cheese, yogurt)
- Nuts and seeds (in large amounts)
- Beans and lentils
- Processed meats (hot dogs, bacon, deli meats)
- Colas and dark sodas

It's essential to monitor phosphorus intake and avoid foods that are either high in phosphorus or contain added phosphorus (such as phosphates in processed foods).

High-Sodium Foods

Sodium increases blood pressure and fluid retention, putting extra strain on the kidneys. To follow a renal diet, it's essential to limit sodium intake. Avoid foods such as:
- Canned soups and vegetables
- Processed meats (ham, sausages, pepperoni)
- Fast food and take-out
- Salted snacks (chips, pretzels)
- Frozen meals and prepackaged meals

Instead, focus on fresh, whole foods and cook meals at home whenever possible to control sodium levels.

High-Protein Foods

Although protein is necessary for the body, excessive amounts can put stress on the kidneys. High-protein foods that should be limited include:
- Red meats (beef, pork, lamb)
- Processed meats (bacon, sausage)
- Full-fat dairy products

Protein intake should be carefully managed, and portion control is key to avoid overburdening the kidneys.

Tips for Navigating the Renal Diet

Read Labels Carefully: Processed foods often contain hidden sources of sodium, phosphorus, and potassium. Always check the nutrition labels for these ingredients.

Meal Planning: Plan meals ahead of time to ensure you're choosing foods that align with your renal diet needs. This will also help you avoid the temptation to grab something high in sodium or potassium when you're hungry.

Portion Control: Even with kidney-friendly foods, portion control is important. Too much of even the healthiest food can overwhelm the kidneys.

Consult Your Healthcare Provider: Each person with kidney disease has unique dietary needs. It's important to work with a healthcare provider or dietitian to tailor the renal diet to your specific situation.

Meal Planning and Preparation

Meal planning is crucial for managing a renal diet effectively. It ensures you have balanced, kidney-friendly meals ready, reduces the risk of dietary slip-ups, and helps maintain overall health. Here's how to plan meals for a renal diet:

Understanding Nutrient Needs
Balance: Aim for meals that balance protein, carbohydrates, and fats while adhering to limitations on sodium, potassium, and phosphorus.
Portion Control: Use appropriate portion sizes to manage nutrient intake and avoid overloading the kidneys.

Creating a Meal Plan
Weekly Planning: Develop a weekly meal plan that includes a variety of foods from all the allowed categories. This helps ensure you receive a range of nutrients while keeping meals interesting.
Shopping List: Prepare a shopping list based on your meal plan to avoid impulse purchases and ensure you have all necessary ingredients.

Recipe Selection
Kidney-Friendly Recipes: Choose recipes that align with dietary restrictions. Look for low-sodium, low-potassium, and low-phosphorus options. Experiment with herbs and spices to add flavor without added salt.
Batch Cooking: Consider preparing meals in advance to save time and ensure you always have kidney-friendly options available.

Cooking Techniques
Healthy Cooking Methods: Opt for baking, grilling, steaming, or sautéing instead of frying. These methods help retain nutrients and minimize the need for added fats and sodium.
Flavoring Alternatives: Use herbs, spices, and citrus to enhance flavor without relying on salt. Experiment with different combinations to find what you enjoy.

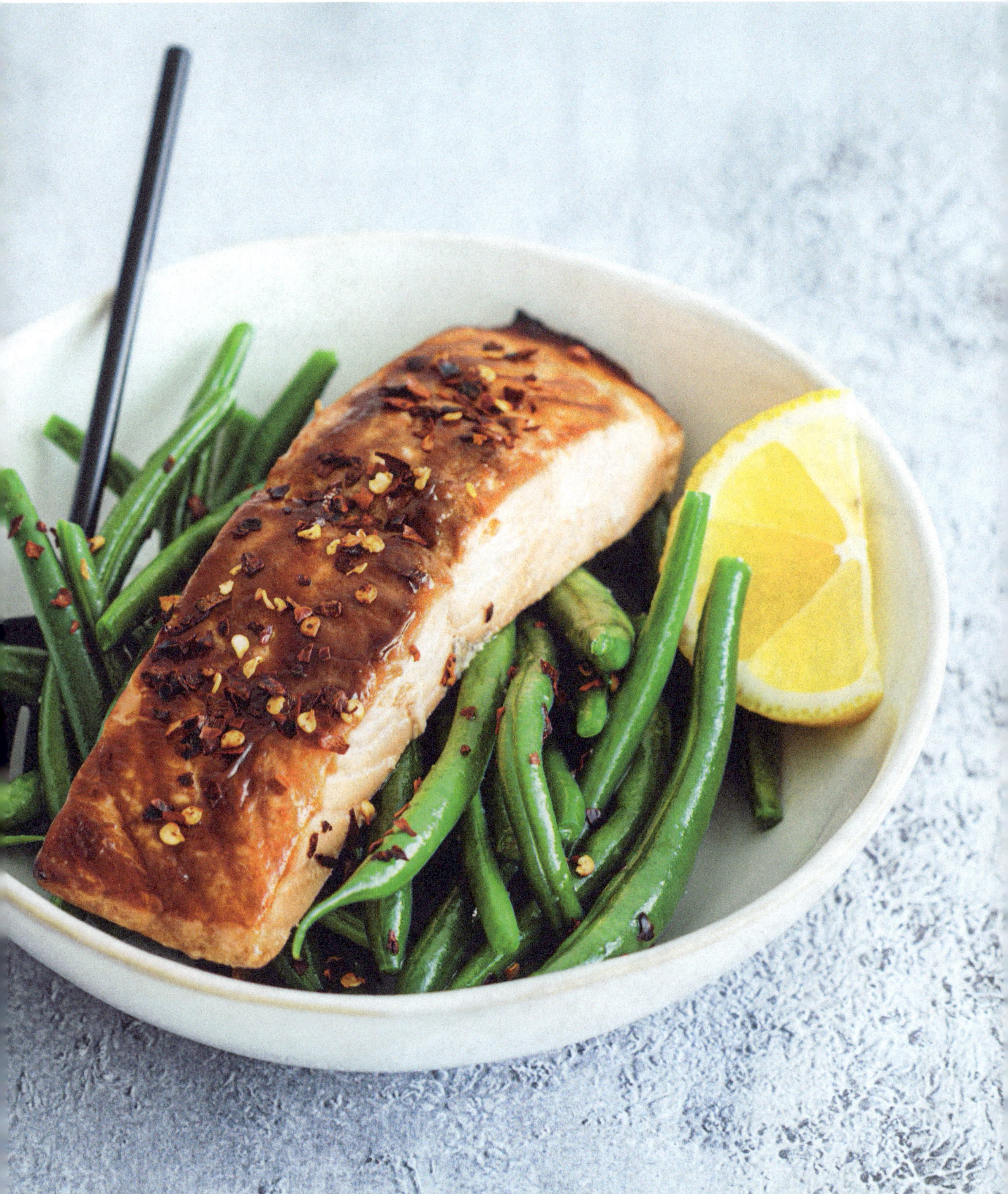

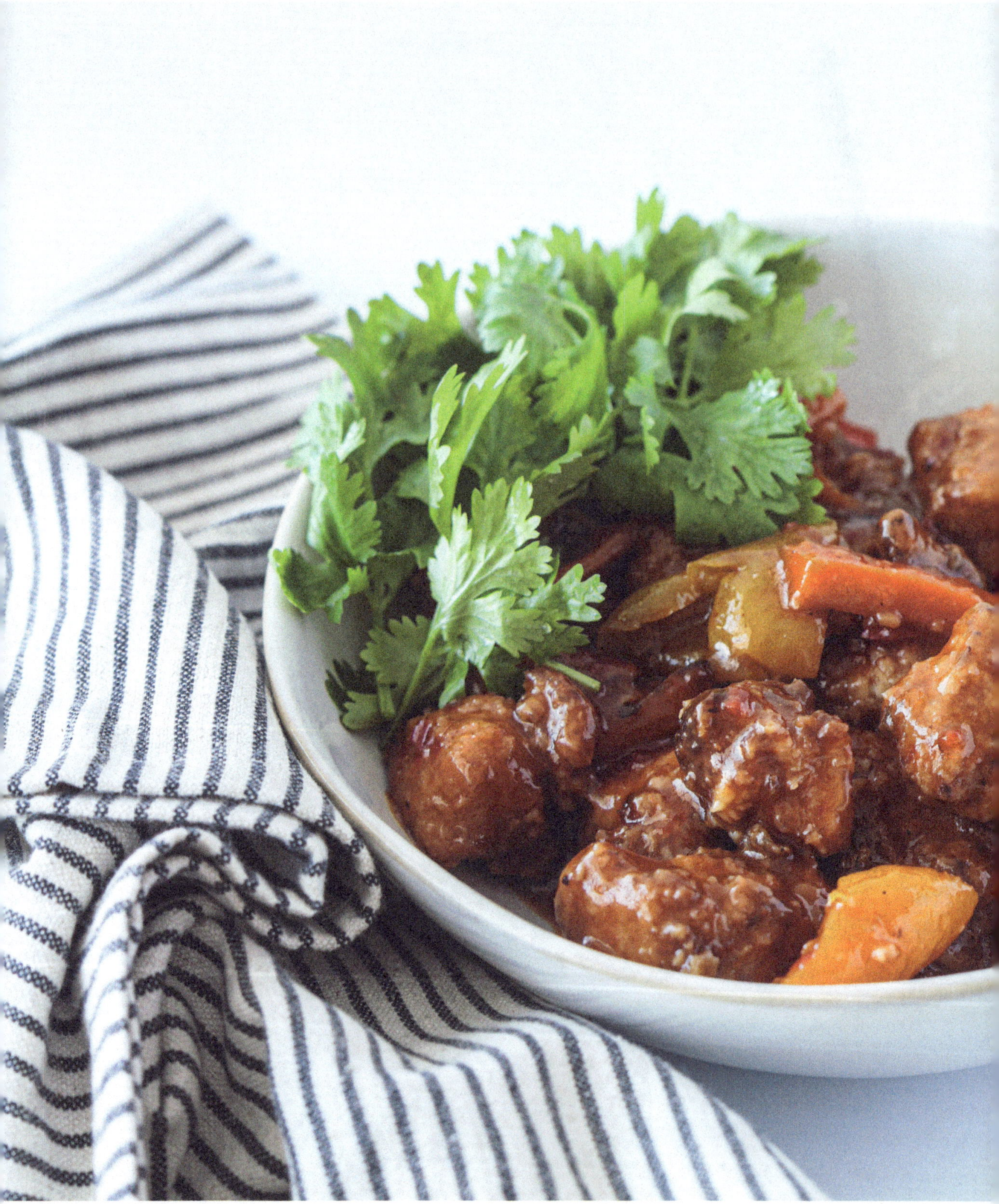

Tips for Successful Meal Preparation

Meal Prepping: Cook and portion meals in advance to make daily preparation easier. Store meals in portion-sized containers for convenience.

Labeling and Storage: Label containers with the date and contents to keep track of freshness and prevent food waste. Store food properly to maintain quality.

Eating Out and Special Occasions: When dining out or attending events, plan ahead. Research restaurant menus for kidney-friendly options and inform hosts about dietary restrictions.

Staying Flexible: Be prepared to adjust your meal plan based on availability of ingredients, changes in health status, or personal preferences.

This book provides a range of recipes specifically designed to fit within the guidelines of a renal diet. However, individual dietary needs can vary significantly based on personal health conditions, stage of kidney disease, and treatment plans. Therefore, while the recipes serve as a valuable resource, each person should adjust their meal plan and recipe choices according to their unique needs. It is essential to consult with a healthcare provider or dietitian to tailor these recipes to your specific dietary requirements. Regular consultations will ensure that your diet remains balanced and effectively supports your kidney health.

BREAKFAST RECIPES

These recipes are carefully designed to align with the principles of the renal diet, offering balanced and kidney-friendly meal options. However, everyone's dietary needs are unique. If you have allergies, intolerances, or your doctor has advised avoiding specific ingredients, feel free to adjust the recipes to suit your individual health requirements. Treat these recipes as a flexible base or inspiration to create meals that work best for you while supporting your kidney health.

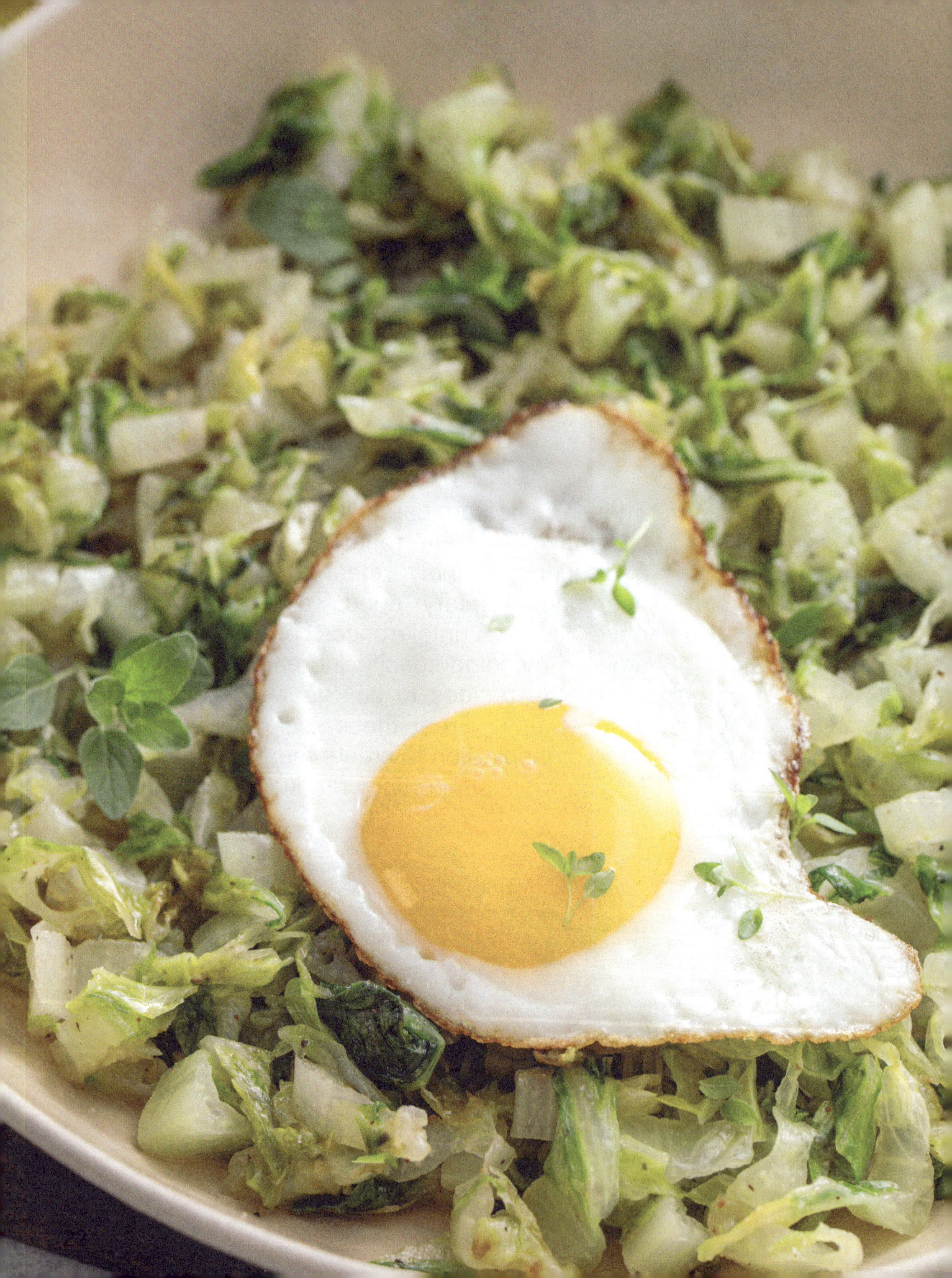

SAUTÉED CABBAGE WITH FRIED EGG

Cooking Difficulty: 2/10

Cooking Time: 18 minutes

Servings: 2

INGREDIENTS

- 2 cups shredded green cabbage
- 1 small onion, thinly sliced
- 2 tablespoons olive oil
- 1 teaspoon garlic powder
- 1/2 teaspoon smoked paprika
- pepper, to taste
- 2 large eggs
- fresh parsley or chives, for garnish (optional)

DESCRIPTION

STEP 1
In a skillet, heat olive oil over medium heat. Add onion and sauté for 3-4 minutes. Stir in cabbage, garlic powder, smoked paprika, and pepper, cooking for 8-10 minutes until tender.

STEP 2
In a separate skillet, fry the eggs to your liking.

STEP 3
Plate the sautéed cabbage and top with a fried egg. Garnish with fresh herbs, if desired. Enjoy!

NUTRITIONAL INFORMATION

146 Calories, 4g Fat, 5g Carbs, 5g Protein

QUINOA BREAKFAST BOWL

Cooking Difficulty: 2/10

Cooking Time: 11 minutes

Servings: 1

INGREDIENTS

- 1/2 cup cooked quinoa
- 1 cup unsweetened almond milk
- 1/2 teaspoon cinnamon
- 1/2 cup mixed berries (blueberries, strawberries, etc.)
- 1 tablespoon sunflower or pumpkin seeds (optional, for garnish)

DESCRIPTION

STEP 1
In a small saucepan, combine the cooked quinoa, almond milk, and cinnamon. Heat over medium heat, stirring occasionally, until it reaches a warm, porridge-like consistency (about 7-9 minutes). Remove from heat and top with the berries and optional sunflower or pumpkin seeds for crunch. Serve warm and enjoy!

NUTRITIONAL INFORMATION

180 Calories, 7g Fat, 15g Carbs, 11g Protein

SALMON MUFFINS

Cooking Difficulty: 2/10	Cooking Time: 22 minutes	Servings: 2

INGREDIENTS

- 2 large eggs
- 1/4 cup unsweetened almond milk
- 50g cooked fresh salmon
- 1 tablespoon olive oil
- 1 tablespoon chopped fresh parsley (optional)
- 2 tablespoons all-purpose flour (or white flour)
- pepper (optional)

DESCRIPTION

STEP 1
Preheat oven to 375°F (190°C) and grease a muffin tin. Whisk eggs, almond milk, olive oil, and flour in a bowl. Fold in flaked salmon and parsley (if using). Pour into 2 muffin cups and bake for 15-20 minutes until firm and golden. Cool slightly before serving.

NUTRITIONAL INFORMATION

130 Calories, 12g Fat, 22g Carbs, 15g Protein

26

OATMEAL WITH BERRIES

Cooking Difficulty: 1/10

Cooking Time: 8 minutes

Servings: 2

INGREDIENTS

- 1 cup rolled oats
- 2 cups unsweetened almond milk
- 1/2 teaspoon vanilla extract (optional)
- 1/2 cup fresh raspberries
- 1/2 cup fresh strawberries, sliced

DESCRIPTION

STEP 1
In a medium saucepan, combine oats, almond milk, and vanilla extract. Bring the mixture to a gentle boil over medium heat, then reduce to low heat and simmer, stirring occasionally, for 5-7 minutes, or until the oats are soft and the oatmeal reaches your desired consistency. Remove from heat and divide the oatmeal between two bowls.

STEP 2
Top each bowl with fresh raspberries, and sliced strawberries. Serve warm, and enjoy!

NUTRITIONAL INFORMATION

258 Calories, 8g Fat, 15g Carbs, 7g Protein

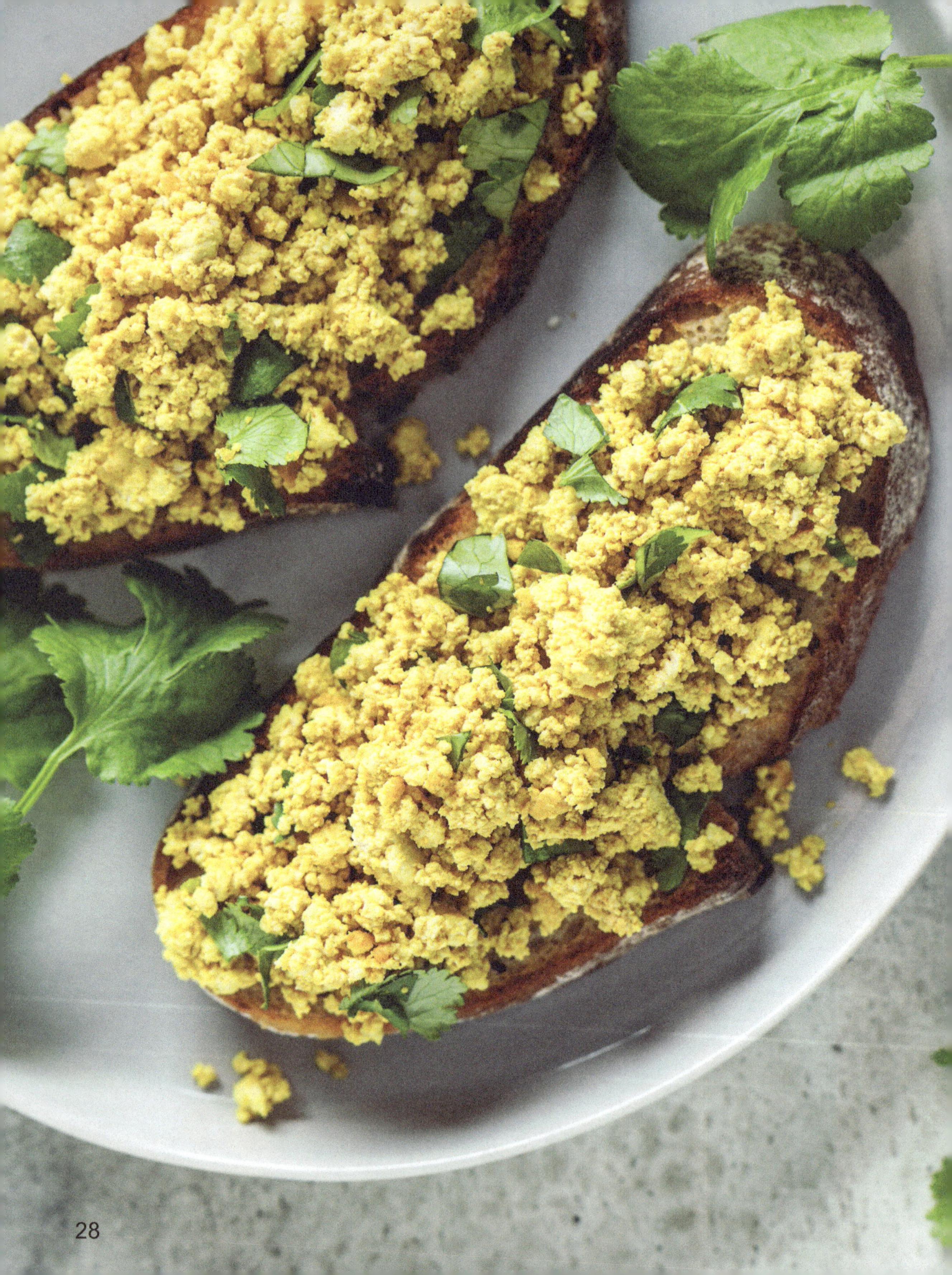

TOFU SCRAMBLE TOAST

Cooking Difficulty: 2/10	Cooking Time: 10 minutes	Servings: 1

INGREDIENTS

- 1 slice white bread (low-sodium)
- 1/3 block firm tofu (about 3 oz), patted dry and crumbled
- 1 teaspoon olive oil
- 1/8 teaspoon ground turmeric
- 1/8 teaspoon smoked paprika
- a pinch of ground cumin
- a pinch of garlic powder
- black pepper, to taste
- 1–2 slices of cucumber or 1 lettuce leaf (optional, for topping)
- fresh cilantro, chopped, for garnish (optional)

DESCRIPTION

STEP 1
Heat the olive oil in a small skillet over medium heat. Add the crumbled tofu and cook for 2–3 minutes, stirring occasionally.

STEP 2
Sprinkle turmeric, smoked paprika, cumin, garlic powder, and black pepper over the tofu. Stir well and cook for another 2 minutes. Toast the slice of white bread.

STEP 3
Place the tofu scramble on the toasted bread. Add cucumber slices or a lettuce leaf on top if desired. Garnish with fresh cilantro and serve immediately.

NUTRITIONAL INFORMATION

200 Calories, 3g Fat, 27g Carbs, 5g Protein

SHRIMP AND EGGS MIX

Cooking Difficulty: 2/10

Cooking Time: 12 minutes

Servings: 2

INGREDIENTS

- 4 large egg whites
- 10 medium shrimp (peeled, deveined, cooked)
- 1 tablespoon olive oil
- 1 small green onion, finely chopped
- 1/4 teaspoon garlic powder
- pepper to taste (optional)
- fresh parsley for garnish (optional)

DESCRIPTION

STEP 1
Heat olive oil in a skillet over medium heat. Add shrimp and green onion, sauté for 1-2 minutes until warm. Whisk egg whites with garlic powder, and pepper. Pour into skillet. Cook, stirring gently, until eggs are set. Garnish with parsley and serve warm.

NUTRITIONAL INFORMATION

227 Calories, 14g Fat, 22g Carbs, 17g Protein

TURMERIC SCRAMBLE

Cooking Difficulty: 2/10

Cooking Time: 7 minutes

Servings: 1

INGREDIENTS

- 2 large egg whites
- 1/4 small red bell pepper, diced
- 2 tablespoons fresh boiled corn kernels (about 1/4 cob)
- 1/4 teaspoon ground turmeric
- 1 tablespoon olive oil
- a pinch of garlic powder (optional)
- pepper to taste

DESCRIPTION

STEP 1

Heat olive oil in a non-stick skillet over medium heat. Add bell pepper and corn, sauté for 2-3 minutes until slightly softened. Whisk egg whites with turmeric, garlic powder, and pepper. Pour egg mixture into the skillet and stir gently until eggs are set and fluffy. Serve warm and enjoy!

NUTRITIONAL INFORMATION

138 Calories, 5g Fat, 11g Carbs, 10g Protein

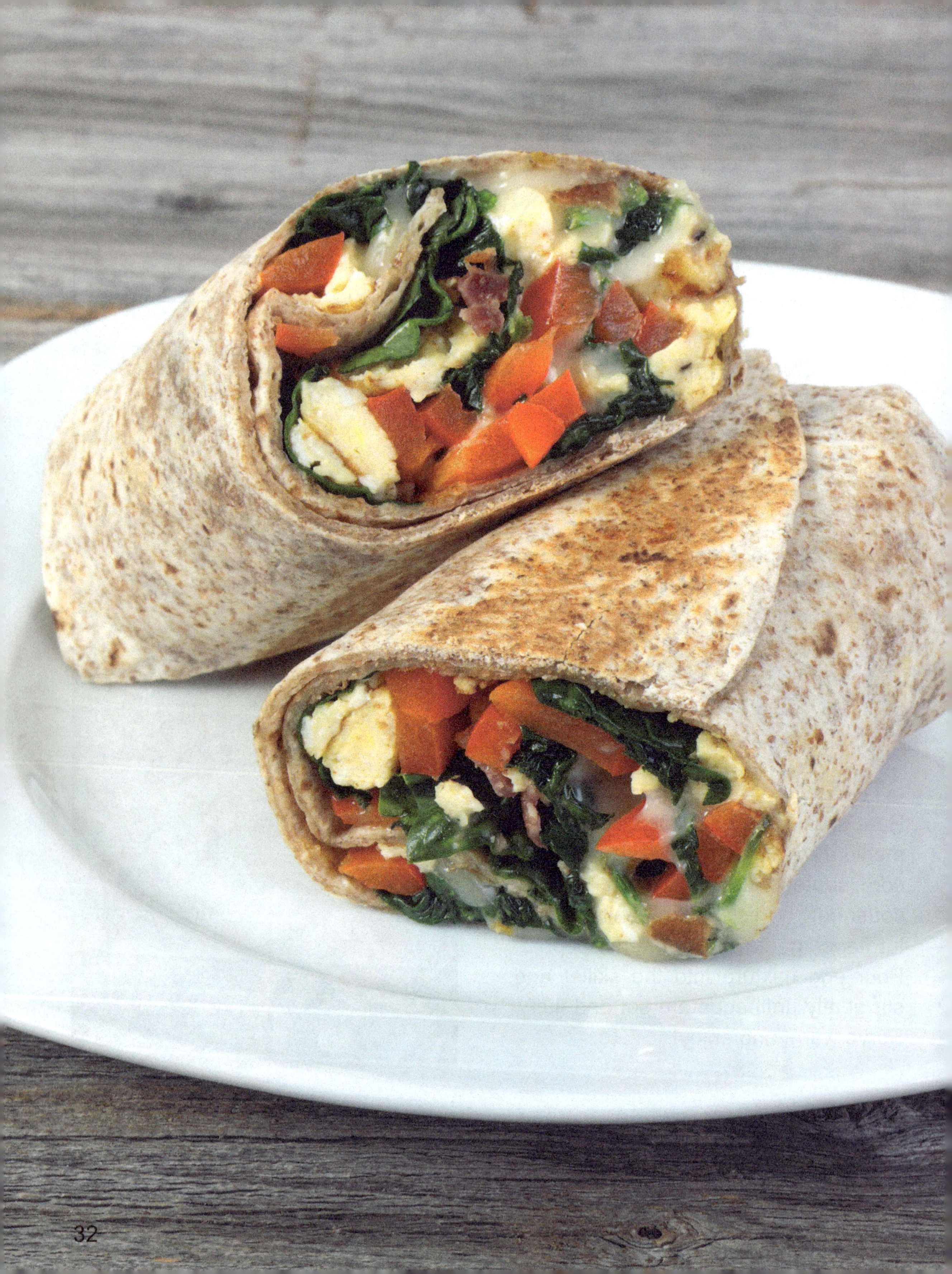

EGG AND VEGETABLE WRAP

Cooking Difficulty: 2/10

Cooking Time: 10 minutes

Servings: 1

INGREDIENTS

- 1 egg + 1 egg white
- 1 small white tortilla (low-sodium, about 8 inches in diameter)
- 1/4 red bell pepper, thinly sliced
- 1/4 cup shredded lettuce
- black pepper to taste
- 1 teaspoon olive oil for cooking

DESCRIPTION

STEP 1
Heat olive oil in a nonstick skillet over medium heat. Add sliced red bell pepper and sauté for 2–3 minutes until softened. Remove from the skillet and set aside.

STEP 2
In the same skillet, scramble the egg and egg white until fully cooked. Warm the tortilla in a dry skillet or microwave. Assemble the wrap by placing the shredded lettuce, cooked vegetables, and scrambled eggs on the tortilla. Season with black pepper to taste.

STEP 3
Roll the tortilla tightly and serve immediately.

NUTRITIONAL INFORMATION

306 Calories, 15g Fat, 25g Carbs, 15g Protein

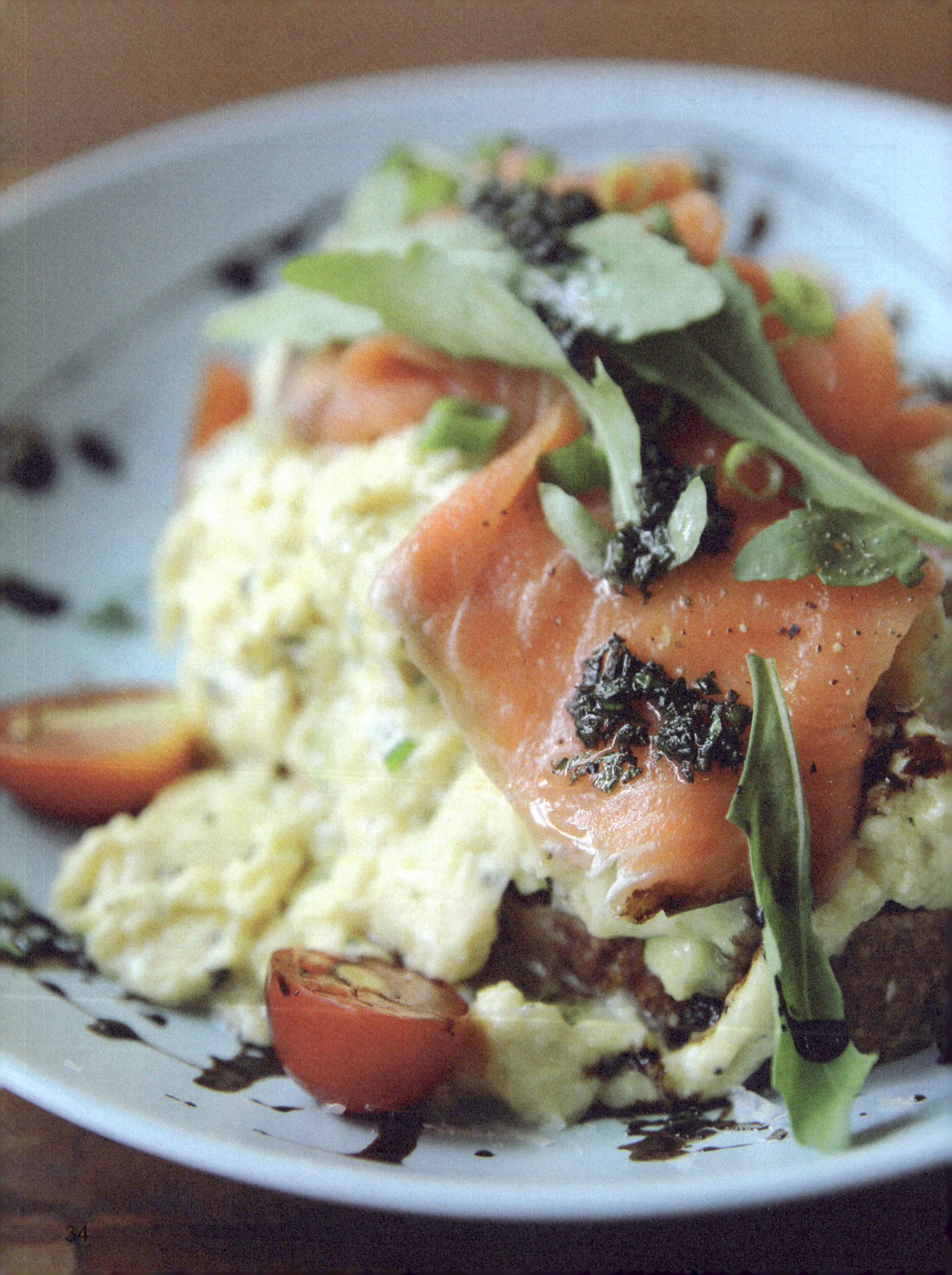

EGG AND SALMON SCRAMBLE

Cooking Difficulty: 2/10
Cooking Time: 10 minutes
Servings: 1

INGREDIENTS

- 2 eggs + 2 egg whites
- 1 tablespoon olive oil
- 50g fresh salmon, diced
- 1/4 red bell pepper, chopped
- 1/4 small tomato, chopped (optional)
- 1 tablespoon green onion, chopped (use sparingly)
- black pepper to taste
- fresh parsley or chives for garnish (optional, small amounts only)

DESCRIPTION

STEP 1
Heat olive oil in a nonstick skillet over medium heat. Add the diced salmon and cook for 2-3 minutes, stirring occasionally, until lightly cooked. Remove from the skillet and set aside.

STEP 2
In the same skillet, sauté the chopped red bell pepper, green onion, and tomato for 2-3 minutes until softened. In a bowl, whisk the eggs and egg whites together. Pour the mixture into the skillet with the vegetables. Stir gently and cook until the eggs are scrambled and fully set. Add the cooked salmon back into the skillet and mix well. Season with black pepper to taste.

STEP 3
Garnish with fresh parsley or chives, if desired, and serve immediately.

NUTRITIONAL INFORMATION

280 Calories, 18g Fat, 4g Carbs, 20g Protein

CUCUMBER, RADISH, AND EGG SALAD

| Cooking Difficulty: 1/10 | Cooking Time: 3 minutes | Servings: 1 |

INGREDIENTS

- 2 egg
- 1/2 small cucumber, diced
- 2-3 radishes, thinly sliced
- 1 teaspoon olive oil
- 1 tablespoon fresh parsley, chopped (optional)
- pepper to taste (optional)

DESCRIPTION

STEP 1
Boil or scramble the egg whites until fully cooked. In a bowl, combine diced cucumber, sliced radishes, and chopped parsley. Add the cooked egg whites and drizzle with olive oil. Season with pepper to taste (optional). Toss gently and serve.

NUTRITIONAL INFORMATION

107 Calories, 4g Fat, 7g Carbs, 5g Protein

CUCUMBER AND BERRY SMOOTHIE

| Cooking Difficulty: 1/10 | Cooking Time: 3 minutes | Servings: 2 |

INGREDIENTS

- 1/2 cucumber, peeled and chopped
- 1/2 cup fresh or frozen strawberries
- 1/2 cup fresh or frozen blueberries
- 1/2 cup unsweetened almond milk
- 1 tablespoon chia seeds (optional)
- ice cubes (optional)

DESCRIPTION

STEP 1
Place the cucumber, strawberries, blueberries, and almond milk in a blender. Add chia seeds and ice cubes if desired. Blend until smooth and creamy. Pour into two glasses and serve immediately.

NUTRITIONAL INFORMATION

78 Calories, 1g Fat, 4g Carbs, 5g Protein

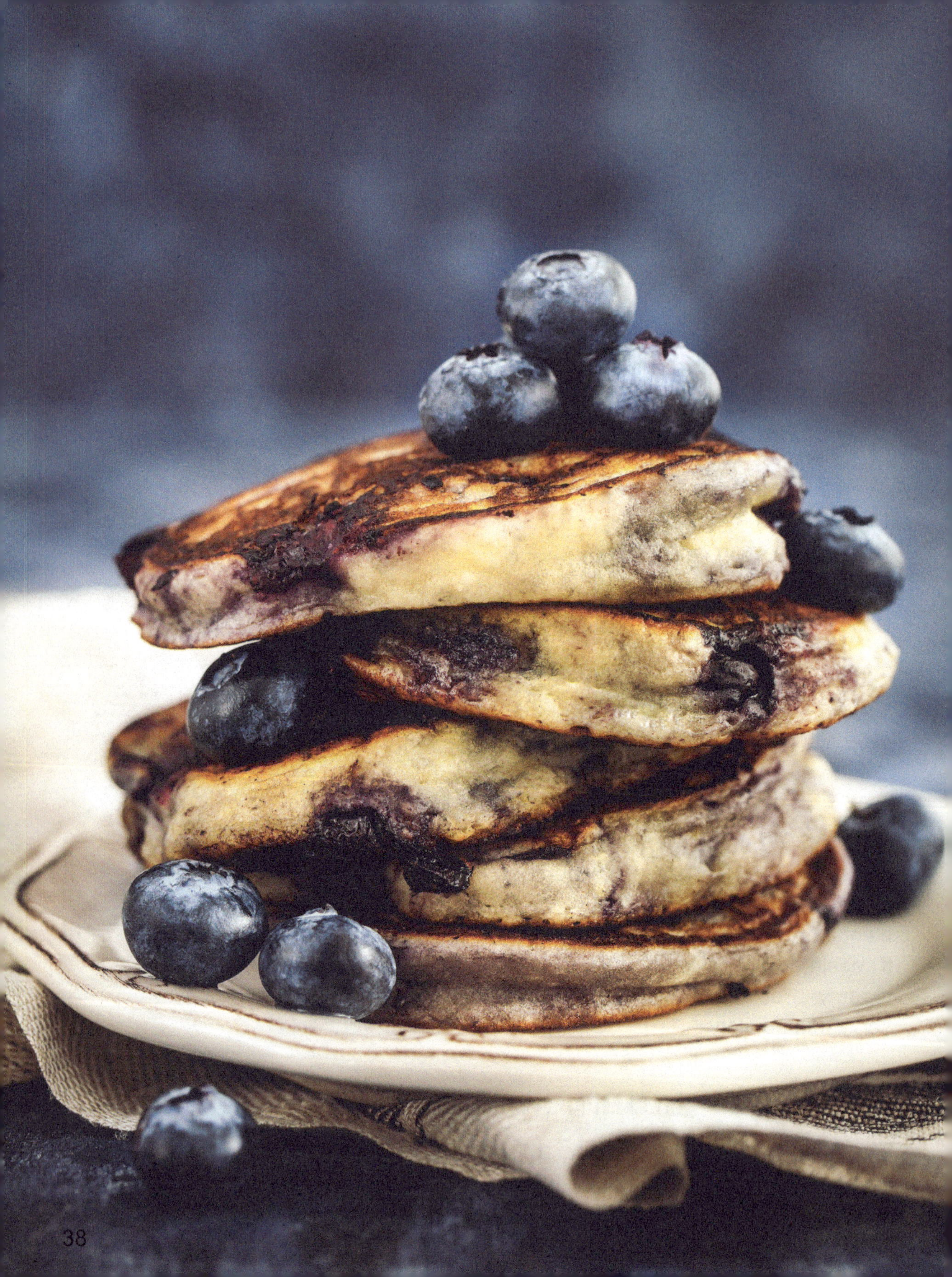

BLUEBERRY PANCAKES

Cooking Difficulty: 2/10

Cooking Time: 26 minutes

Servings: 2

INGREDIENTS

- 1/2 cup whole wheat flour (low in potassium)
- 1/2 cup unsweetened almond milk (or rice milk)
- 1 egg white
- 1/2 teaspoon baking powder
- 1/4 teaspoon vanilla extract
- 1/4 teaspoon cinnamon
- 1/2 cup fresh blueberries
- 1 teaspoon maple syrup (optional)
- olive oil or cooking spray (for cooking)

DESCRIPTION

STEP 1
In a mixing bowl, whisk together the flour, baking powder, cinnamon, and vanilla extract. In a separate bowl, whisk the egg white and almond milk until combined.

STEP 2
Pour the wet ingredients into the dry ingredients and stir until smooth. If the batter is too thick, add a little more almond milk to reach the desired consistency. Gently fold in the blueberries. Heat a nonstick skillet over medium heat and lightly grease with olive oil or cooking spray. Pour small amounts of batter into the skillet to form pancakes. Cook for 2-3 minutes on each side, until golden brown. Serve with a drizzle of maple syrup (optional).

NUTRITIONAL INFORMATION

200 Calories, 3g Fat, 27g Carbs, 5g Protein

MAIN DISH

These recipes are carefully designed to align with the principles of the renal diet, offering balanced and kidney-friendly meal options. However, everyone's dietary needs are unique. If you have allergies, intolerances, or your doctor has advised avoiding specific ingredients, feel free to adjust the recipes to suit your individual health requirements. Treat these recipes as a flexible base or inspiration to create meals that work best for you while supporting your kidney health.

42

BAKED SALMON WITH TZATZIKI SAUCE

Cooking Difficulty: 2/10

Cooking Time: 20 minutes

Servings: 1

INGREDIENTS

for the salmon:
- 1 small salmon steak (about 3-4 oz)
- 1 teaspoon olive oil
- 1/4 teaspoon dried dill
- pepper to taste (optional)

for the tzatziki sauce:
- 1/4 cup plain greek yogurt (unsweetened, low-sodium)
- 1/4 small cucumber, finely grated and drained
- 1/2 teaspoon lemon juice
- 1/4 teaspoon garlic powder (optional)
- 1/4 teaspoon dried dill

DESCRIPTION

STEP 1
Preheat the oven to 375°F (190°C). Rub the salmon steak with olive oil, dill, and a pinch of pepper. Place on a parchment-lined baking sheet and bake for 12-15 minutes, or until cooked through and flaky.

STEP 2
In a small bowl, mix Greek yogurt, grated cucumber, lemon juice, garlic powder (if using), and dill. Stir until well combined.

STEP 3
Plate the baked salmon alongside a bed of salad greens. Spoon the tzatziki sauce on top of the salmon or serve on the side.

NUTRITIONAL INFORMATION

310 Calories, 17g Fat, 11g Carbs, 21g Protein

VEGGIE ROAST

| Cooking Difficulty: 1/10 | Cooking Time: 28 minutes | Servings: 2 |

INGREDIENTS

- 1 cup broccoli florets
- 1 cup cauliflower florets
- 2 tablespoons olive oil
- 1/4 teaspoon black pepper
- 1/4 teaspoon paprika

DESCRIPTION

STEP 1
Preheat oven to 400 degrees F (200 degrees C). In a large bowl, toss broccoli, cauliflower, olive oil, salt, pepper, and paprika. Spread vegetables in a single layer on a baking sheet lined with parchment paper. Roast for 20-25 minutes, or until vegetables are tender and slightly crispy.

NUTRITIONAL INFORMATION

157 Calories, 10g Fat, 10g Carbs, 5g Protein

FISH WITH VEGETABLES

Cooking Difficulty: 2/10

Cooking Time: 15 minutes

Servings: 1

INGREDIENTS

- 150 grams white fish fillet (such as cod or haddock)
- 1/2 zucchini, sliced
- 1/2 bell pepper, sliced
- 1/4 red onion, sliced
- 1 tablespoon olive oil
- salt and pepper to taste

DESCRIPTION

STEP 1
Preheat the grill. Cut the zucchini, bell pepper, and onion into bite-sized pieces. Drizzle the fish and vegetables with olive oil, salt, and pepper. Grill the fish for 5-7 minutes per side, or until opaque. Grill the vegetables for 3-5 minutes, or until tender. Serve the fish with the grilled vegetables.

NUTRITIONAL INFORMATION

250 Calories, 12g Fat, 4g Carbs, 30g Protein

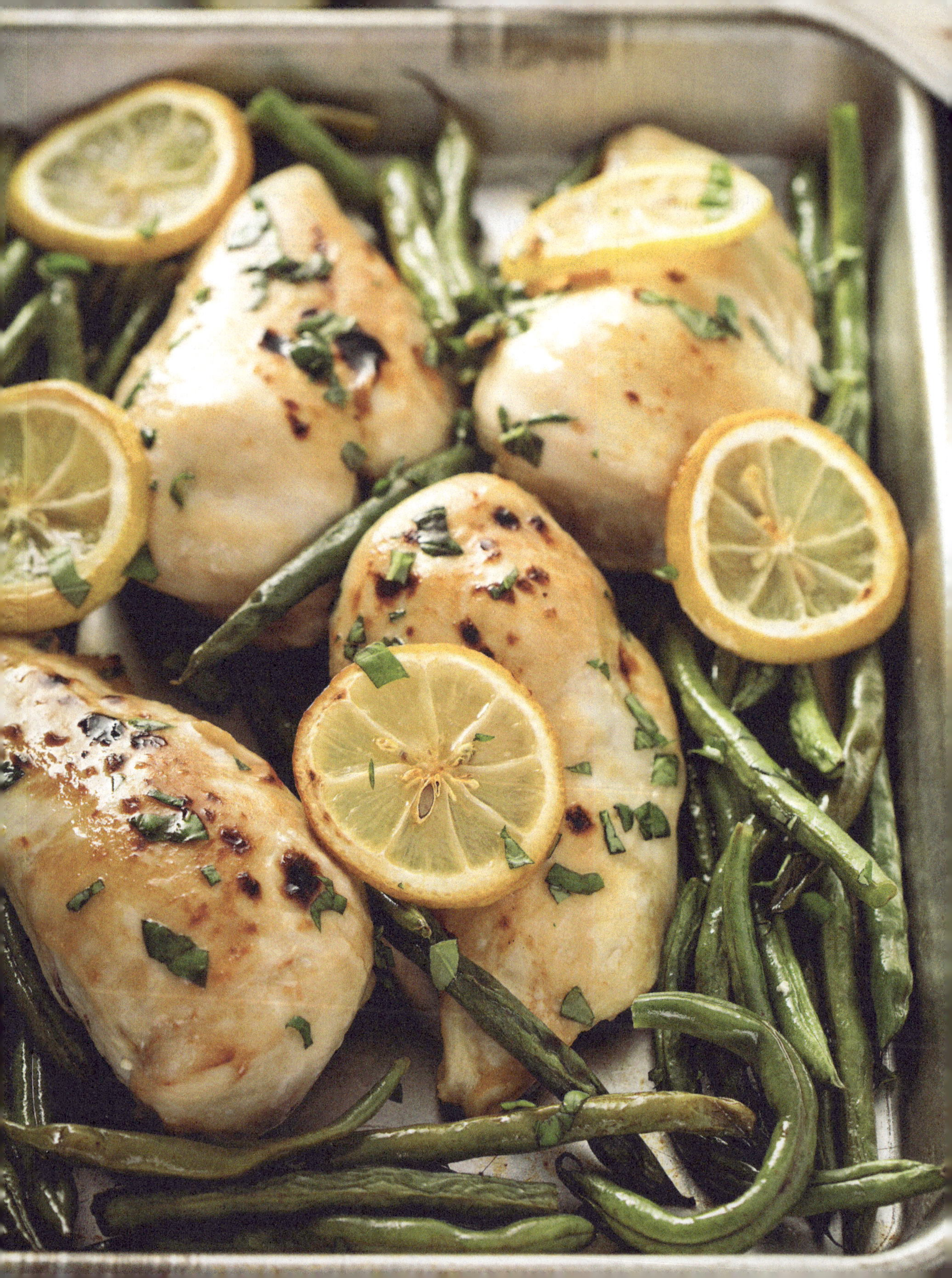

LEMON HERB BAKED CHICKEN

Cooking Difficulty: 2/10

Cooking Time: 45 minutes

Servings: 4

INGREDIENTS

- 4 boneless, skinless chicken breasts (about 3 lbs)
- 2 tablespoons olive oil
- 1 tablespoon lemon juice
- 1 teaspoon dried oregano
- 1/2 teaspoon dried thyme
- 1/4 teaspoon garlic powder
- 1/4 teaspoon paprika
- freshly ground black pepper to taste
- 1 pound (450 g) green beans, trimmed and cut into bite-sized pieces
- 1 lemon, thinly sliced

DESCRIPTION

STEP 1
Preheat your oven to 400°F (200°C). In a small bowl, whisk together olive oil, lemon juice, oregano, thyme, garlic powder, paprika, and pepper.

STEP 2
Place chicken breasts in a baking dish. Pour the marinade over the chicken, ensuring they're evenly coated. Arrange the green beans around the chicken breasts. Top with lemon slices.

STEP 3
Bake for 30-35 minutes, or until the chicken is cooked through. Let the chicken rest for a few minutes before serving.

NUTRITIONAL INFORMATION

300 Calories, 15g Fat, 17g Carbs, 25g Protein

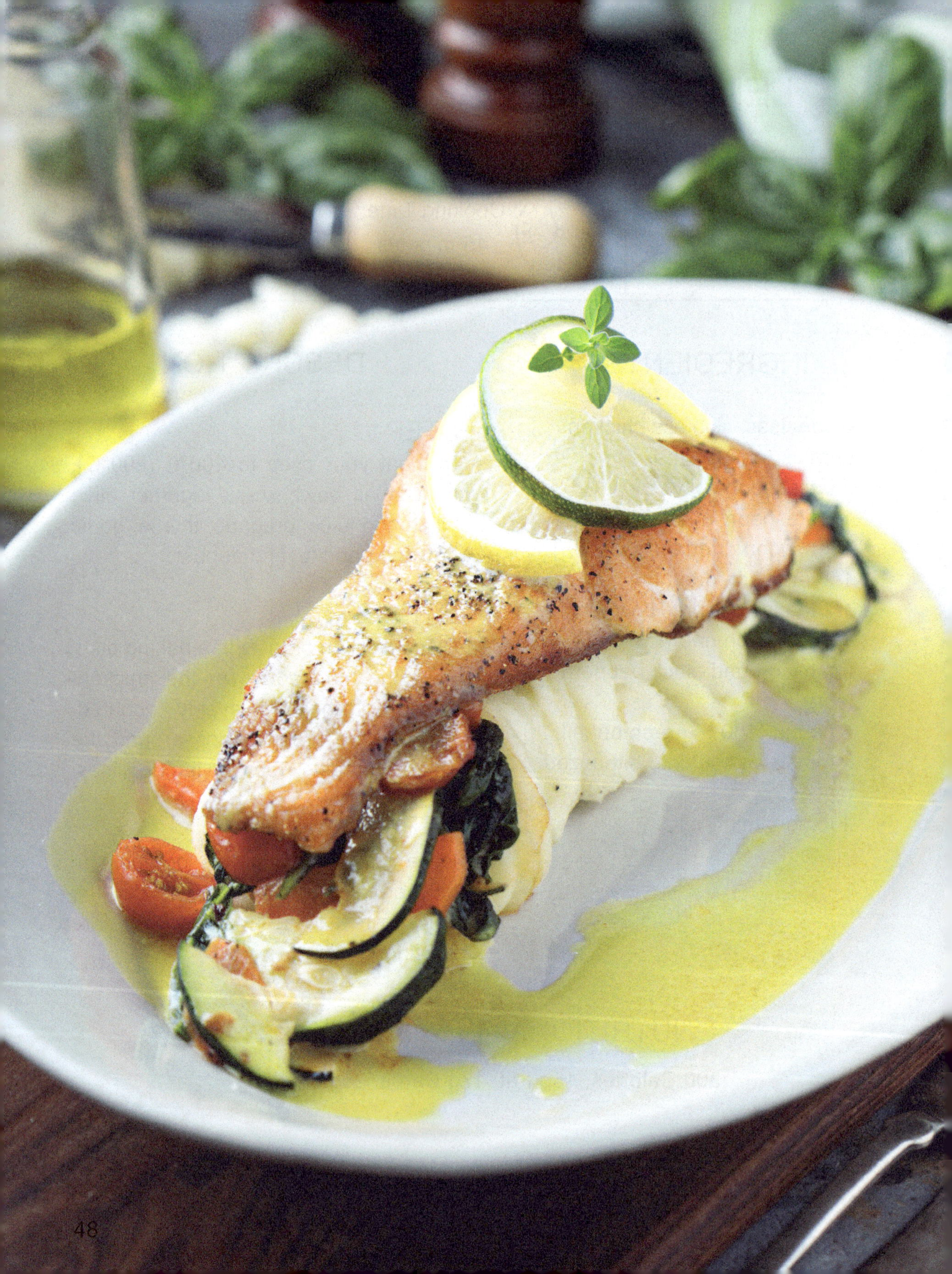

BAKED SALMON WITH LEMON AND HERBS

Cooking Difficulty: 2/10

Cooking Time: 25 minutes

Servings: 2

INGREDIENTS

- 2 salmon fillets (about 6 ounces each)
- 1 tablespoon olive oil
- 1/4 teaspoon black pepper
- 1/4 teaspoon dried oregano
- 1/4 teaspoon dried thyme
- 1 lemon, thinly sliced (optional)

DESCRIPTION

STEP 1
Preheat oven to 400 degrees F (200 degrees C). Line a baking sheet with parchment paper.

STEP 2
In a small bowl, combine olive oil, pepper, oregano, and thyme. Place salmon fillets on the prepared baking sheet and spread the spice mixture evenly over them. Top with lemon slices, if using.

STEP 3
Bake for 15-20 minutes, or until salmon is cooked through. Serve baked salmon with your favorite vegetables.

NUTRITIONAL INFORMATION

230 Calories, 10g Fat, 10g Carbs, 5g Protein

ZUCCHINI FRITTERS

Cooking Difficulty: 2/10 | Cooking Time: 18 minutes | Servings: 2

INGREDIENTS

- 1 medium zucchini, grated
- 1 egg
- 2 tablespoonswhole wheat flour (low in potassium)
- 1 tablespoon chopped fresh herbs (dill, parsley, cilantro)
- 1 clove garlic, minced
- 1/4 teaspoon black pepper
- olive oil for frying

DESCRIPTION

STEP 1
Grate the zucchini and squeeze out excess moisture. In a bowl, combine zucchini, egg, flour, herbs, garlic, and pepper. Heat oil in a skillet over medium heat. Drop spoonfuls of batter into the skillet and cook for 2-3 minutes per side, or until golden brown. Serve warm with your favorite dipping sauce.

NUTRITIONAL INFORMATION

250 Calories, 12g Fat, 4g Carbs, 30g Protein

SALMON WITH BROCCOLI

Cooking Difficulty: 2/10

Cooking Time: 15 minutes

Servings: 1

INGREDIENTS

- 7 oz (200 g) salmon fillet, cut into cubes
- 5 oz (150 g) broccoli florets
- ¼ red onion, diced
- 1 tablespoon olive oil
- ¼ teaspoon black pepper
- 1 tablespoon lemon juice (optional)

DESCRIPTION

STEP 1
Preheat oven to 400°F (200°C). In a bowl, combine salmon, broccoli, red onion, olive oil, and pepper. Spread mixture on a baking sheet lined with parchment paper. Bake for 15-20 minutes, or until salmon is opaque and broccoli is tender. Drizzle with lemon juice before serving, if desired.

NUTRITIONAL INFORMATION

450 Calories, 17g Fat, 20g Carbs, 28g Protein

52

ROASTED TURKEY BREAST

Cooking Difficulty: 2/10
Cooking Time: 28 minutes
Servings: 2

INGREDIENTS

- 1 turkey breast (about 14 ounces)
- 1 tablespoon olive oil
- 1/2 teaspoon black pepper
- 1/2 teaspoon ground coriander
- 1/4 teaspoon ground cumin
- 1/4 teaspoon paprika
- 1/4 teaspoon cayenne pepper (optional)
- 1/4 cup fresh parsley, chopped

DESCRIPTION

STEP 1
Preheat oven to 400 degrees F (200 degrees C). In a small bowl, combine olive oil, pepper, coriander, cumin, paprika, and cayenne pepper (optional).

STEP 2
Rub the spice mixture all over the turkey breast. Place the turkey breast on a baking sheet lined with parchment paper. Roast for 20-25 minutes, or until the turkey is cooked through.

STEP 3
Sprinkle with parsley and serve.

NUTRITIONAL INFORMATION

350 Calories, 15g Fat, 5g Carbs, 40g Protein

COD WITH VEGETABLES

Cooking Difficulty: 2/10
Cooking Time: 25 minutes
Servings: 2

INGREDIENTS

- 2 cod fillets (about 5 oz each)
- 1 zucchini, diced
- 1 bell pepper, diced
- 1/4 red onion, diced
- 1 tablespoon olive oil
- 1 tablespoon lemon juice
- 1 teaspoon dried oregano
- 1/4 teaspoon black pepper

DESCRIPTION

STEP 1
Preheat oven to 400 degrees F (200 degrees C). In a bowl, whisk together olive oil, lemon juice, oregano, and pepper. Add cod fillets, zucchini, bell pepper, and red onion to the marinade. Toss to coat. Arrange mixture on a baking sheet lined with parchment paper. Bake for 15-20 minutes.

NUTRITIONAL INFORMATION

280 Calories, 17g Fat, 8g Carbs, 18g Protein

CHICKEN WITH VEGETABLES

Cooking Difficulty: 2/10

Cooking Time: 23 minutes

Servings: 2

INGREDIENTS

- 7 oz (200 g) chicken breast, cut into cubes
- 1/2 zucchini, diced
- 1/2 bell pepper, diced
- 1/4 red onion, diced
- 1 tablespoon olive oil
- pepper to taste

DESCRIPTION

STEP 1

Heat olive oil in a large skillet over medium heat. Add chicken and cook until golden brown and cooked through, about 5-7 minutes per side. Add zucchini, bell pepper, and red onion to the pan. Cook for an additional 5-7 minutes, or until vegetables are tender-crisp. Season with pepper to taste. Serve immediately.

NUTRITIONAL INFORMATION

350 Calories, 15g Fat, 10g Carbs, 30g Protein

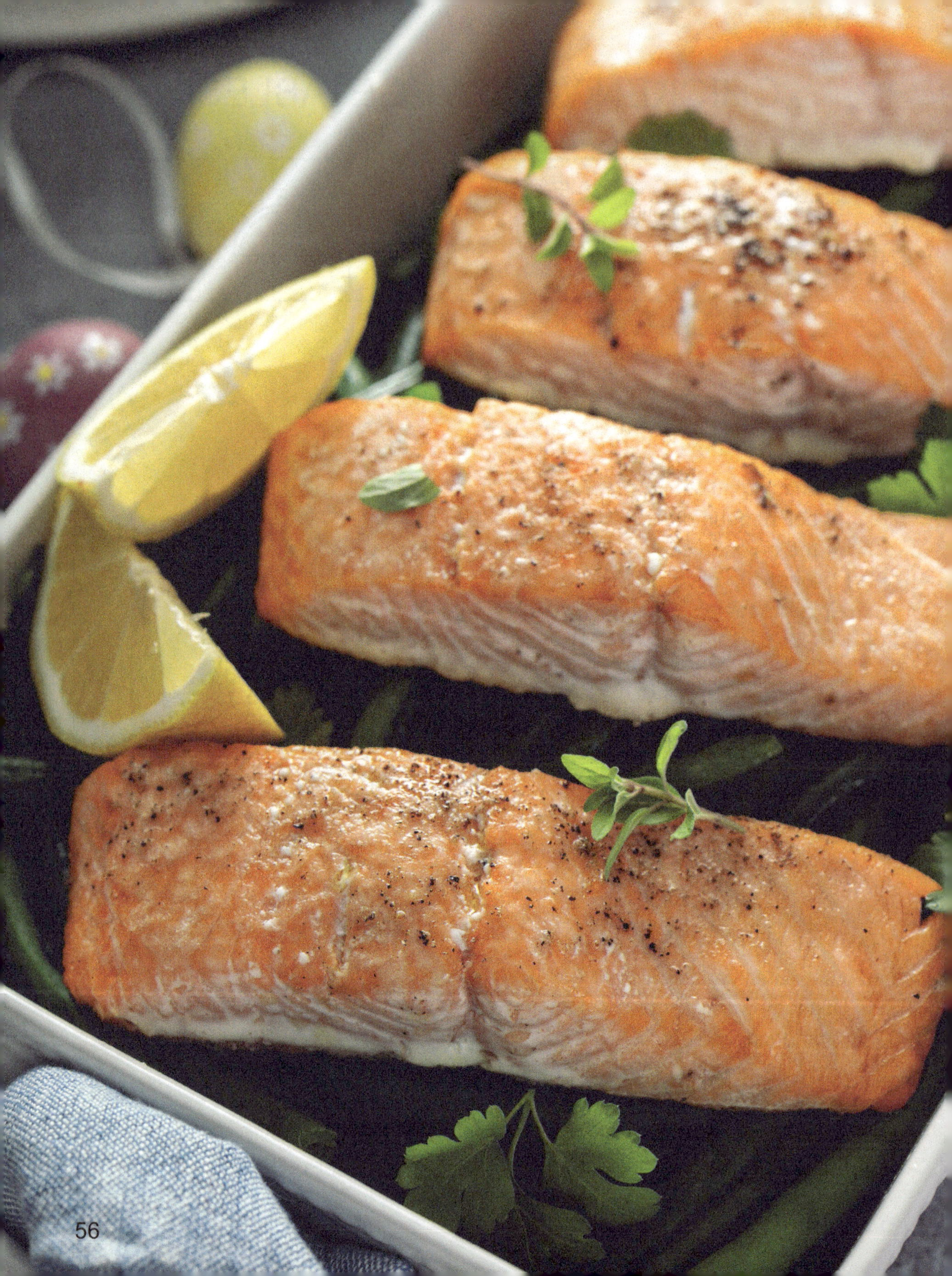

BAKED SALMON WITH GREEN BEANS

Cooking Difficulty: 2/10

Cooking Time: 25 minutes

Servings: 4

INGREDIENTS

- 4 salmon fillets (about 5.5 ounces each)
- 14 ounces green beans, trimmed
- 1 tablespoon olive oil
- 1/4 teaspoon black pepper
- 1 lemon, sliced
- 1/4 cup fresh parsley, chopped

DESCRIPTION

STEP 1
Preheat oven to 400 degrees F (200 degrees C). Wash and trim the green beans. Blanch in boiling water for 2-3 minutes, then drain and set aside.
In a large bowl, toss the green beans with olive oil, and pepper.

STEP 2
Spread the green beans in a baking dish. Place the salmon fillets on top of the green beans. Season the salmon with pepper, and lemon slices. Bake for 15-20 minutes, or until the salmon is cooked through. Garnish with parsley and serve.

NUTRITIONAL INFORMATION

400 Calories, 17g Fat, 10g Carbs, 38g Protein

CHICKEN PATTIES

Cooking Difficulty: 2/10	Cooking Time: 28 minutes	Servings: 2

INGREDIENTS

- 10.5 oz ground chicken
- 2.5 oz green onion, chopped
- ¼ cup (1/2 onion) finely chopped
- 1 egg
- 2 tablespoons rolled oats
- 1 tablespoon olive oil
- pepper to taste

DESCRIPTION

STEP 1
Preheat oven to 350°F (180°C). In a bowl, combine chicken, green onion, onion, egg, oats, olive oil, and pepper. Shape mixture into 2 meatballs. Place meatballs on a baking sheet lined with parchment paper. Bake for 20-25 minutes, or until meatballs are cooked through.

NUTRITIONAL INFORMATION

350 Calories, 15g Fat, 10g Carbs, 30g Protein

RADISH AND CUCUMBER SALAD

| Cooking Difficulty: 1/10 | Cooking Time: 4 minutes | Servings: 1 |

INGREDIENTS

- 6 radishes, thinly sliced
- 1/2 cup fresh or frozen green peas blanched if frozen (optional)
- 1/2 cucumber, diced
- 1 tablespoon fresh dill, chopped
- 1 tablespoon olive oil
- juice of 1 lime

DESCRIPTION

STEP 1

In a large bowl, combine sliced radishes, green peas, diced cucumber, and chopped dill. In a small bowl, whisk together olive oil, and lime juice if desired. Drizzle the dressing over the salad and toss gently to combine. Divide between two plates and serve immediately.

NUTRITIONAL INFORMATION

105 Calories, 2g Fat, 3g Carbs, 1g Protein

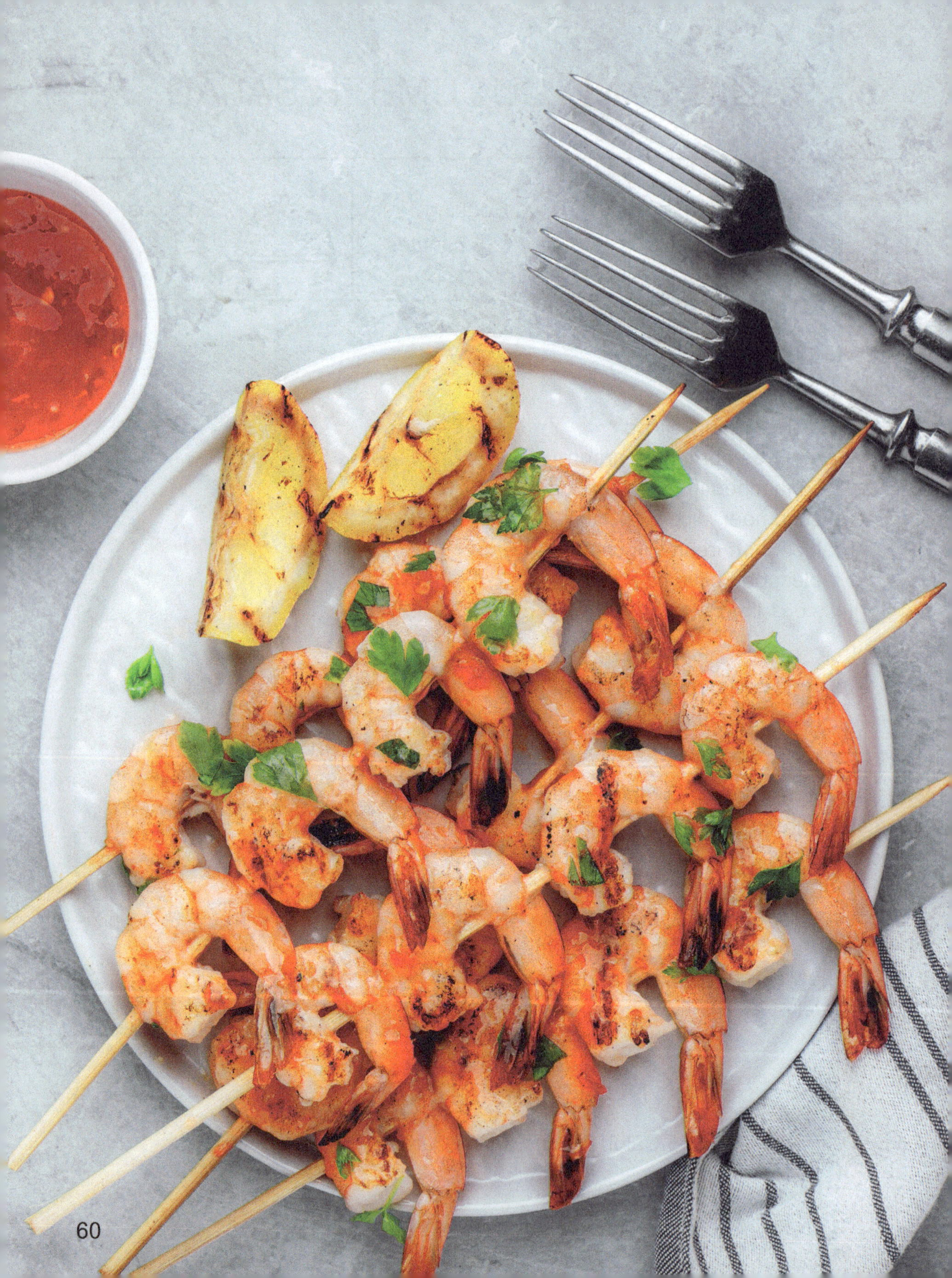

GRILLED SHRIMP SKEWERS

| Cooking Difficulty: 2/10 | Cooking Time: 27 minutes | Servings: 4 |

INGREDIENTS

- 1 pound large shrimp, tails on and unpeeled
- ¼ cup olive oil
- 2 tablespoons lime juice
- 1 tablespoon minced garlic
- 1 teaspoon dried oregano
- ¼ teaspoon black pepper
- ¼ cup chopped fresh parsley (optional)

DESCRIPTION

STEP 1
In a medium bowl, whisk together olive oil, lime juice, garlic, oregano, and pepper. Add shrimp and toss to coat. Cover and refrigerate for 30 minutes, or up to 2 hours.

STEP 2
Preheat grill pan or grill to medium heat. Thread shrimp onto skewers, leaving tails on. Grill for 2-3 minutes per side, or until shrimp are pink and opaque.

STEP 3
Serve shrimp skewers immediately with lemon wedges, fresh herbs, your favorite vegetables, and salad greens.

NUTRITIONAL INFORMATION

200 Calories, 12g Fat, 4g Carbs, 22g Protein

LENTIL SOUP

| Cooking Difficulty: 2/10 | Cooking Time: 35 minutes | Servings: 2 |

INGREDIENTS

- 1 cup lentils, rinsed
- 4 cups low-sodium vegetable broth
- 1 onion, chopped
- 1 carrot, diced
- 1 celery stalk, diced
- 1/2 teaspoon dried thyme
- 1/4 teaspoon black pepper
- fresh parsley, chopped

DESCRIPTION

STEP 1
In a large pot, sauté onion, carrot, and celery in a small amount of olive oil until softened. Add lentils, vegetable broth, thyme, and black pepper. Bring to a boil, then reduce heat and simmer for 25-30 minutes, or until lentils are tender. Serve hot, garnished with fresh parsley.

NUTRITIONAL INFORMATION

110 Calories, 5g Fat, 7g Carbs, 7g Protein

CREAMY CAULIFLOWER SOUP

| Cooking Difficulty: 2/10 | Cooking Time: 15 minutes | Servings: 2 |

INGREDIENTS

- 1 medium head of cauliflower
- 1 onion
- 2 cloves garlic
- 1 quart vegetable broth (low-sodium)
- 2 tablespoons olive oil
- pepper to taste
- fresh herbs for garnish

DESCRIPTION

STEP 1
Chop cauliflower into florets, and finely chop onion and garlic. Sauté onion and garlic in olive oil until softened. Add cauliflower and broth. Simmer until cauliflower is tender. Puree soup until smooth using an immersion blender. Season with pepper. Garnish with fresh herbs.

NUTRITIONAL INFORMATION

120 Calories, 3g Fat, 5g Carbs, 7g Protein

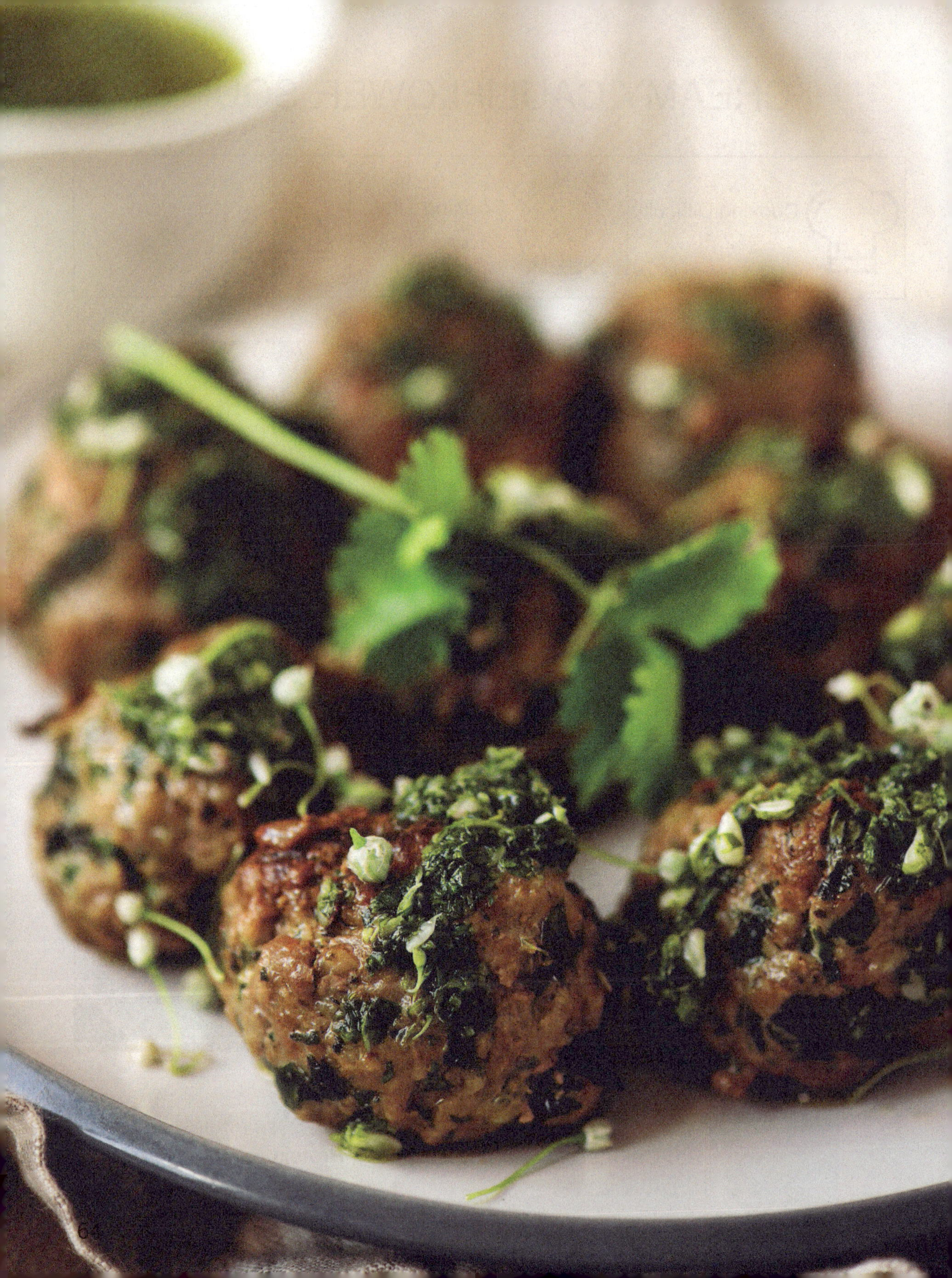

TURKEY MEATBALLS WITH MINT

Cooking Difficulty: 2/10

Cooking Time: 27 minutes

Servings: 4

INGREDIENTS

- 1 pound ground turkey
- 1/2 onion, finely chopped
- 1 clove garlic, minced
- 1/4 cup fresh mint, chopped
- 1 egg
- 1/4 cup bread crumbs
- 1 tablespoon olive oil
- 1/4 teaspoon black pepper
- 1/4 teaspoon nutmeg

DESCRIPTION

STEP 1
Preheat oven to 350 degrees F (175 degrees C). In a large bowl, combine turkey, onion, garlic, mint, egg, bread crumbs, olive oil, pepper, and nutmeg.

STEP 2
Shape the mixture into 1-inch meatballs. Place meatballs on a baking sheet lined with parchment paper. Bake for 20-25 minutes, or until meatballs are browned and cooked through.

STEP 3
Serve immediately with your favorite sauce and vegetables.

NUTRITIONAL INFORMATION

327 Calories, 18g Fat, 10g Carbs, 28g Protein

ZUCCHINI AND CARROT RIBBON SALAD

| Cooking Difficulty: 1/10 | Cooking Time: 8 minutes | Servings: 2 |

INGREDIENTS

- 1 medium zucchini, peeled into thin ribbons
- 1 medium carrot, peeled into thin ribbons
- 1 tablespoon olive oil
- 1 teaspoon lemon juice
- fresh parsley, chopped (for garnish)

DESCRIPTION

STEP 1
Use a vegetable peeler to create thin ribbons of zucchini and carrot. Toss the ribbons with olive oil and lemon juice in a bowl. Garnish with fresh parsley and serve.

NUTRITIONAL INFORMATION

70 Calories, 6g Fat, 5g Carbs, 1g Protein

CABBAGE AND CUCUMBER SALAD

| Cooking Difficulty: 1/10 | Cooking Time: 4 minutes | Servings: 2 |

INGREDIENTS

- 1 cup green cabbage, finely shredded
- 1/2 cup cucumber, diced
- 1 tablespoon olive oil
- 1 teaspoon apple cider vinegar
- fresh dill, chopped (for garnish)
- pepper to taste

DESCRIPTION

STEP 1
Combine shredded cabbage and cucumber in a bowl. Drizzle with olive oil and apple cider vinegar. Mix well. Garnish with fresh dill and serve immediately.

NUTRITIONAL INFORMATION

80 Calories, 6g Fat, 5g Carbs, g Protein

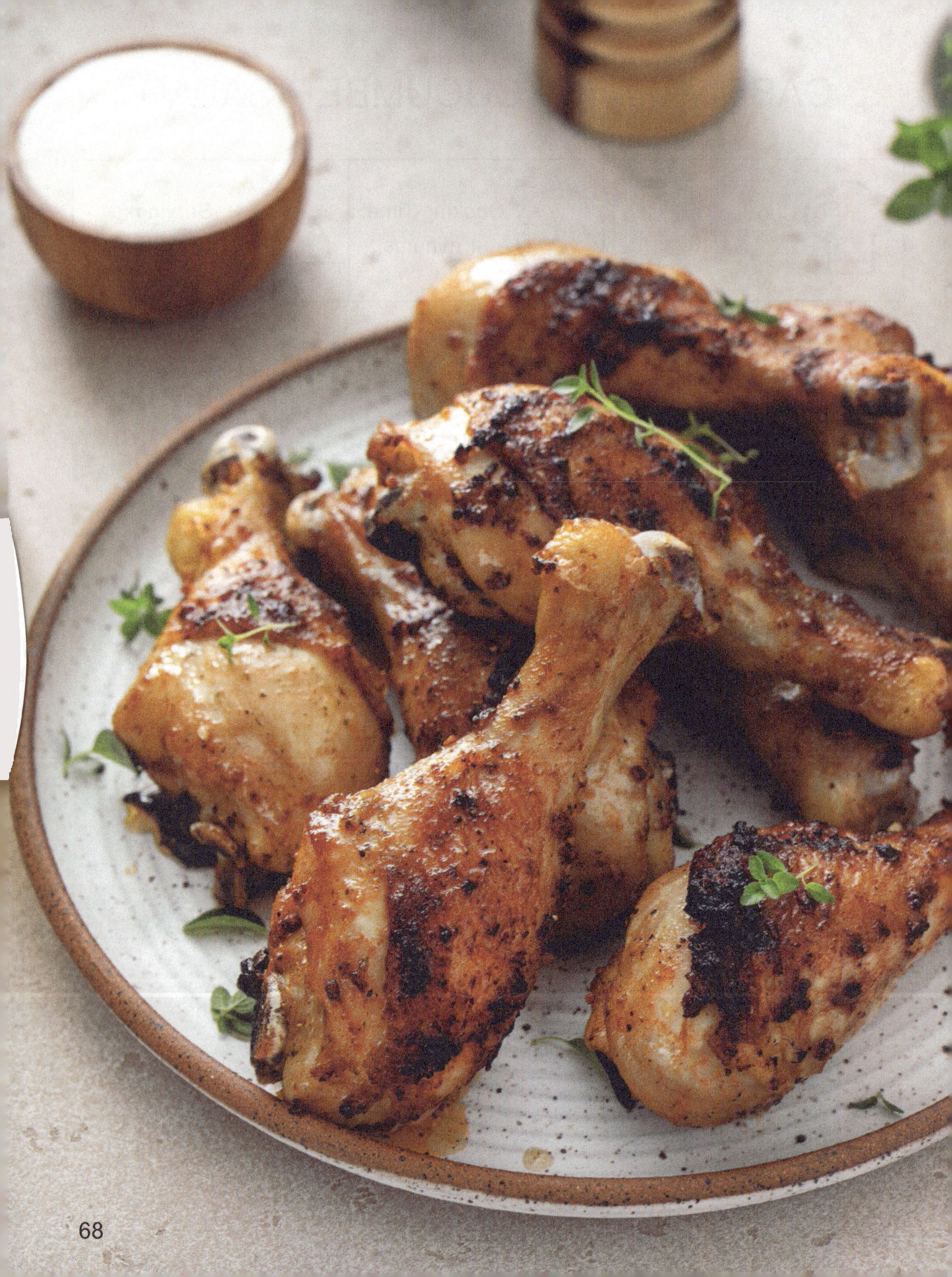

BAKED CHICKEN LEGS

Cooking Difficulty: 2/10

Cooking Time: 57 minutes

Servings: 4

INGREDIENTS

- 4 bone-in, skin-on chicken legs
- 1/4 cup olive oil
- 2 tablespoons lemon juice
- 1 tablespoon dried oregano
- 1 teaspoon dried thyme
- 1/4 teaspoon black pepper
- 1/4 cup chopped fresh parsley
- 2 cloves garlic, minced
- 1 teaspoon sweet paprika

DESCRIPTION

STEP 1
Preheat oven to 400°F (200°C). Whisk together olive oil, lemon juice, oregano, thyme, pepper, paprika, parsley, and garlic in a large bowl. Add chicken legs and toss to coat. Marinate for at least 30 minutes, or up to 4 hours in the refrigerator.

STEP 2
Arrange chicken legs in a single layer in a baking dish. Pour marinade over chicken. Bake for 40-50 minutes, or until cooked through and skin is crispy. Garnish with parsley and serve alongside vegetables.

NUTRITIONAL INFORMATION

400 Calories, 20g Fat, 5g Carbs, 25g Protein

SHRIMP AND GREEN BEAN SALAD

| Cooking Difficulty: 2/10 | Cooking Time: 10 minutes | Servings: 2 |

INGREDIENTS

- 1 cup green beans, steamed
- 8-10 shrimp, boiled and peeled
- 1 tablespoon olive oil
- 1 teaspoon fresh lemon juice
- black pepper, to taste
- fresh parsley, chopped (optional)

DESCRIPTION

STEP 1
Combine steamed green beans and boiled shrimp in a bowl. Drizzle with olive oil and lemon juice. Sprinkle with black pepper and parsley. Toss gently. Serve immediately as a light, renal-friendly salad.

NUTRITIONAL INFORMATION

120 Calories, 5g Fat, 7g Carbs, 14g Protein

ARUGULA AND CUCUMBER SALAD

| | Cooking Difficulty: 1/10 | | Cooking Time: 5 minutes | | Servings: 2 |

INGREDIENTS

- 2 cups fresh arugula
- 1/2 cup cucumber, diced
- 1 tablespoon olive oil
- 1 teaspoon fresh lemon juice
- 1 teaspoon fresh dill, chopped
- black pepper, to taste

DESCRIPTION

STEP 1
In a bowl, combine arugula and diced cucumber. Drizzle with olive oil and lemon juice. Sprinkle with fresh dill and a pinch of black pepper. Toss gently and serve immediately as a light, renal-friendly salad.

NUTRITIONAL INFORMATION

75 Calories, 6g Fat, 5g Carbs, 1,5g Protein

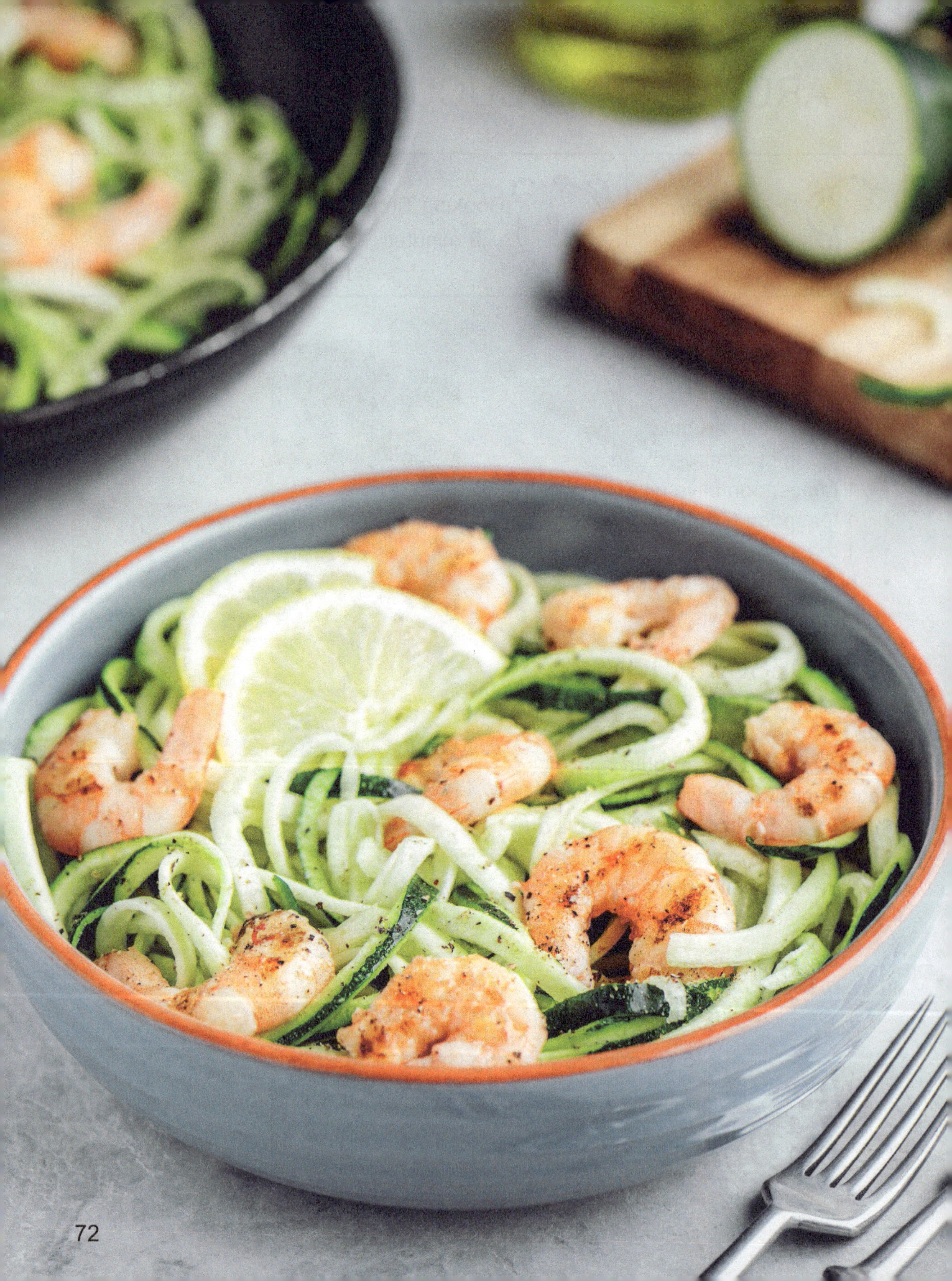

ZUCCHINI SHRIMP SPAGHETTI

Cooking Difficulty: 2/10
Cooking Time: 17 minutes
Servings: 2

INGREDIENTS

- 2 medium zucchinis, spiralized
- 10 medium shrimp, peeled and deveined
- 1 tablespoon olive oil
- 1 garlic clove, minced (optional)
- 1/4 teaspoon dried oregano
- 1/4 teaspoon paprika
- juice of 1/2 lemon
- pepper to taste (optional)
- fresh parsley, chopped, for garnish

DESCRIPTION

STEP 1
Heat olive oil in a skillet over medium heat. Add shrimp, garlic, oregano, and paprika. Cook for 2-3 minutes per side until the shrimp are pink and cooked through.

STEP 2
Add the spiralized zucchini to the skillet and sauté for 2-3 minutes until just tender. Squeeze lemon juice over the shrimp and zucchini. Season with pepper if desired.

STEP 3
Divide between two plates, garnish with fresh parsley, and serve immediately.

NUTRITIONAL INFORMATION

273 Calories, 11g Fat, 15g Carbs, 15g Protein

GREEN BEANS WITH LEMON-HERB

| Cooking Difficulty: 1/10 | Cooking Time: 7 minutes | Servings: 2 |

INGREDIENTS

- 2 cups fresh green beans, trimmed
- 1 tablespoon olive oil
- 1 teaspoon fresh lemon juice
- 1/2 teaspoon garlic powder
- 1 teaspoon fresh parsley, chopped
- 1/2 teaspoon dried oregano
- a pinch of black pepper (optional)

DESCRIPTION

STEP 1
Steam the green beans for 4-5 minutes until tender but crisp. In a small bowl, whisk together olive oil, lemon juice, garlic powder, parsley, oregano, and black pepper. Toss the warm green beans with the sauce to coat evenly. Serve immediately.

NUTRITIONAL INFORMATION

85 Calories, 5g Fat, 7g Carbs, 2g Protein

LEMON GARLIC GRILLED CHICKEN

| Cooking Difficulty: 2/10 | Cooking Time: 20 minutes | Servings: 2 |

INGREDIENTS

- 2 small chicken fillets (4-5 oz each)
- 1 tablespoon olive oil
- 1 teaspoon lemon juice
- 1 garlic clove, minced
- black pepper, to taste
- fresh parsley, chopped (optional)

DESCRIPTION

STEP 1
In a bowl, mix olive oil, lemon juice, minced garlic, and black pepper. Coat the chicken fillets in the marinade and let sit for 10 minutes. Heat a grill pan over medium heat and grill the chicken for 4-5 minutes per side or until fully cooked. Garnish with parsley and serve with your favorite vegetables.

NUTRITIONAL INFORMATION

180 Calories, 7g Fat, 1g Carbs, 24g Protein

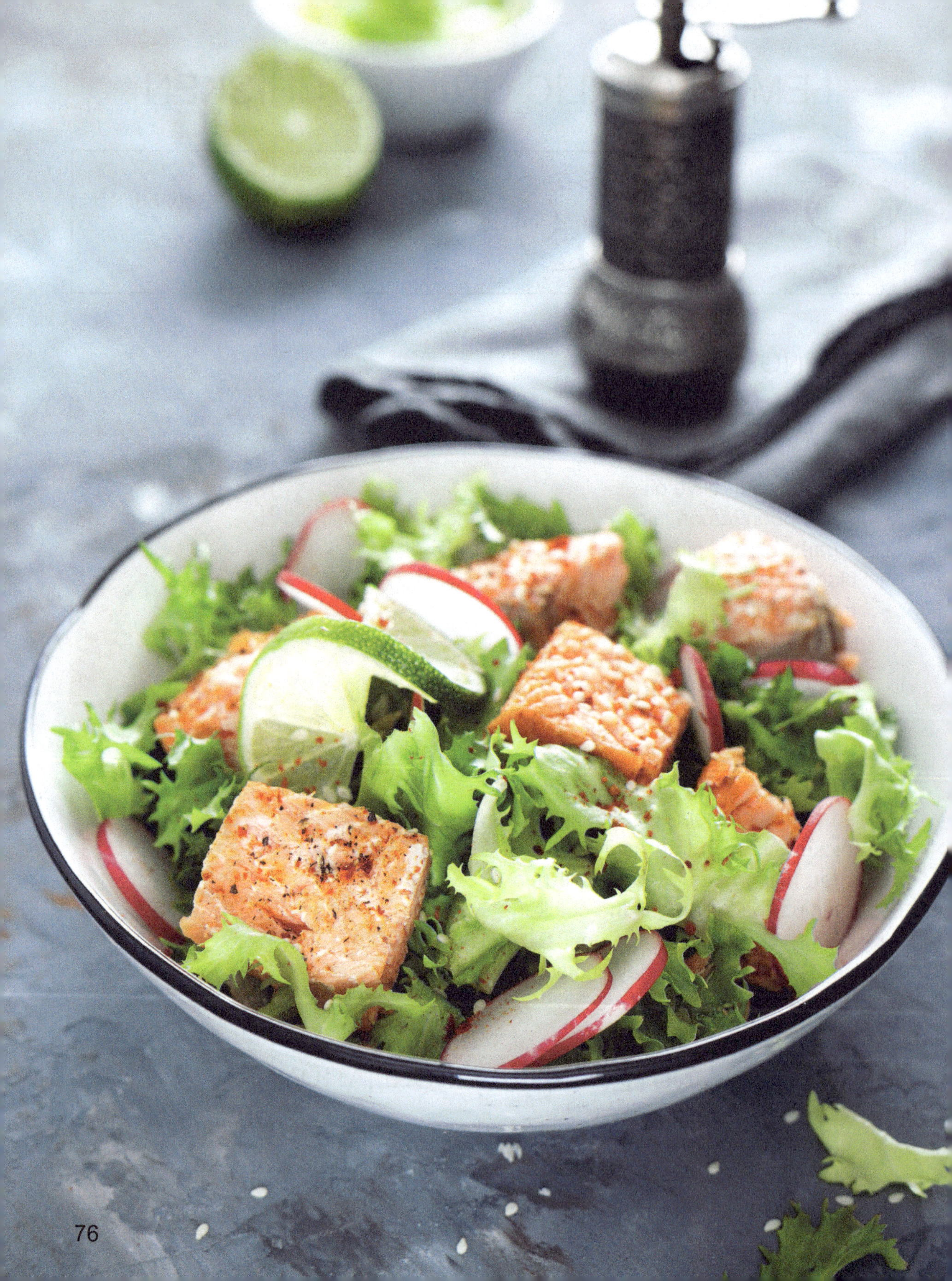

SALMON SALAD WITH LIME DRESSING

Cooking Difficulty: 1/10
Cooking Time: 18 minutes
Servings: 2

INGREDIENTS

- 1 small salmon fillet (about 4 oz)
- 2 cups mixed salad greens (e.g., lettuce or arugula)
- 4 radishes, thinly sliced
- 1 tablespoon olive oil
- juice of 1 lime
- pepper to taste (optional)

DESCRIPTION

STEP 1
Preheat the oven to 375°F (190°C). Place the salmon fillet on a baking sheet lined with parchment paper. Bake for 12-15 minutes, or until cooked through. Let cool slightly, then cut into cubes.

STEP 2
In a large bowl, combine the salad greens and sliced radishes. In a small bowl, whisk together olive oil, lime juice, and pepper (if desired).

STEP 3
Add the baked salmon cubes to the salad. Drizzle with the lime dressing and toss gently to combine. Divide between two plates and serve immediately.

NUTRITIONAL INFORMATION

300 Calories, 8g Fat, 5g Carbs, 6g Protein

ZUCCHINI AND GREEN BEAN PASTA

Cooking Difficulty: 1/10

Cooking Time: 17 minutes

Servings: 2

INGREDIENTS

- 1/2 cup cooked low-sodium pasta (like penne or fusilli)
- 1/2 cup zucchini, diced
- 1/4 cup green beans, chopped and steamed
- 1 tablespoon olive oil
- 1 garlic clove, minced
- 1 teaspoon fresh parsley, chopped
- black pepper, to taste

DESCRIPTION

STEP 1
Heat olive oil in a skillet over medium heat. Sauté garlic for 1 minute. Add zucchini and green beans, cooking for 3-4 minutes until tender. Toss in the cooked pasta, stirring gently to combine. Season with black pepper. Garnish with parsley and serve immediately.

NUTRITIONAL INFORMATION

260 Calories, 8g Fat, 30g Carbs, 6g Protein

CHICKEN SKEWERS WITH VEGETABLES

| Cooking Difficulty: 2/10 | Cooking Time: 24 minutes | Servings: 2 |

INGREDIENTS

- 8 oz (2 small) chicken fillets, cut into cubes
- 1/2 cup zucchini, sliced into rounds
- 1/2 cup red bell pepper, cut into chunks
- 1 tablespoon olive oil
- 1 teaspoon lemon juice
- 1/2 teaspoon garlic powder
- black pepper, to taste

DESCRIPTION

STEP 1

Preheat oven to 400°F (200°C) and line a baking sheet. Toss chicken and veggies in olive oil, lemon juice, garlic powder, and pepper. Thread onto skewers and bake for 15-20 minutes, turning halfway. Serve warm with your favorite steamed vegetables.

NUTRITIONAL INFORMATION

240 Calories, 7g Fat, 6g Carbs, 28g Protein

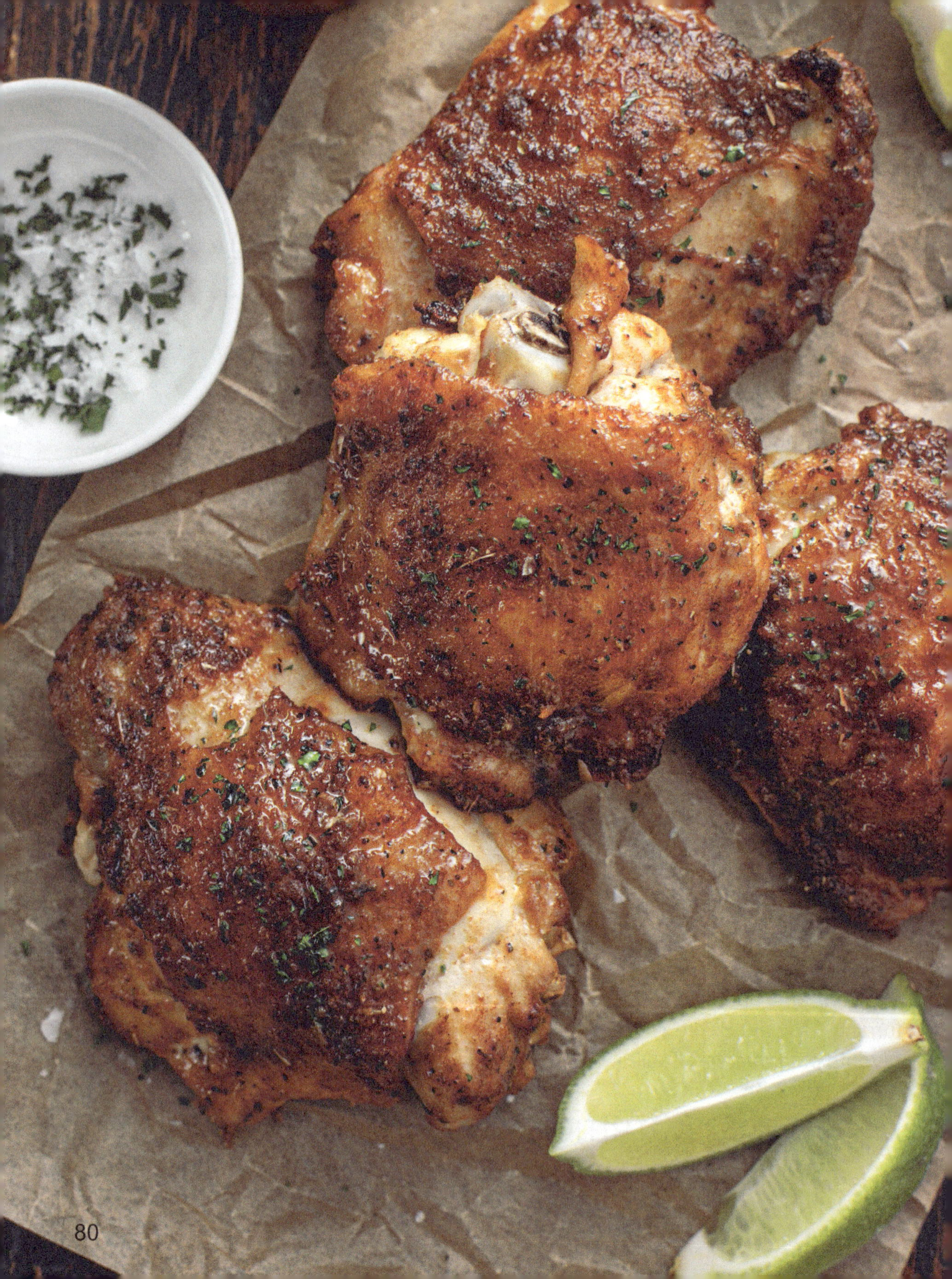

CHICKEN THIGHS WITH HERBS

Cooking Difficulty: 2/10

Cooking Time: 47 minutes

Servings: 4

INGREDIENTS

- 4 chicken thighs (about 1 pound)
- 2 tablespoons olive oil
- 1/2 teaspoon black pepper
- 1/2 teaspoon paprika
- 1/4 teaspoon garlic powder
- 1/4 teaspoon onion powder
- 1/4 teaspoon smoked paprika
- 1/4 teaspoon ground cumin
- 1/8 teaspoon cayenne pepper (optional)
- 1/4 cup fresh parsley, chopped

DESCRIPTION

STEP 1
Preheat oven to 400 degrees F (200 degrees C). In a small bowl, combine olive oil, pepper, paprika, garlic powder, onion powder, smoked paprika, cumin, and cayenne pepper (optional). Rub the spice mixture all over the chicken thighs.

STEP 2
Place the chicken thighs on a baking sheet lined with parchment paper. Roast for 35-45 minutes, or until the chicken is cooked through and the juices run clear. Garnish with parsley and serve alongside vegetables.

NUTRITIONAL INFORMATION

377 Calories, 19g Fat, 15g Carbs, 25g Protein

SNACKS & DESSERTS

These recipes are carefully designed to align with the principles of the renal diet, offering balanced and kidney-friendly meal options. However, everyone's dietary needs are unique. If you have allergies, intolerances, or your doctor has advised avoiding specific ingredients, feel free to adjust the recipes to suit your individual health requirements. Treat these recipes as a flexible base or inspiration to create meals that work best for you while supporting your kidney health.

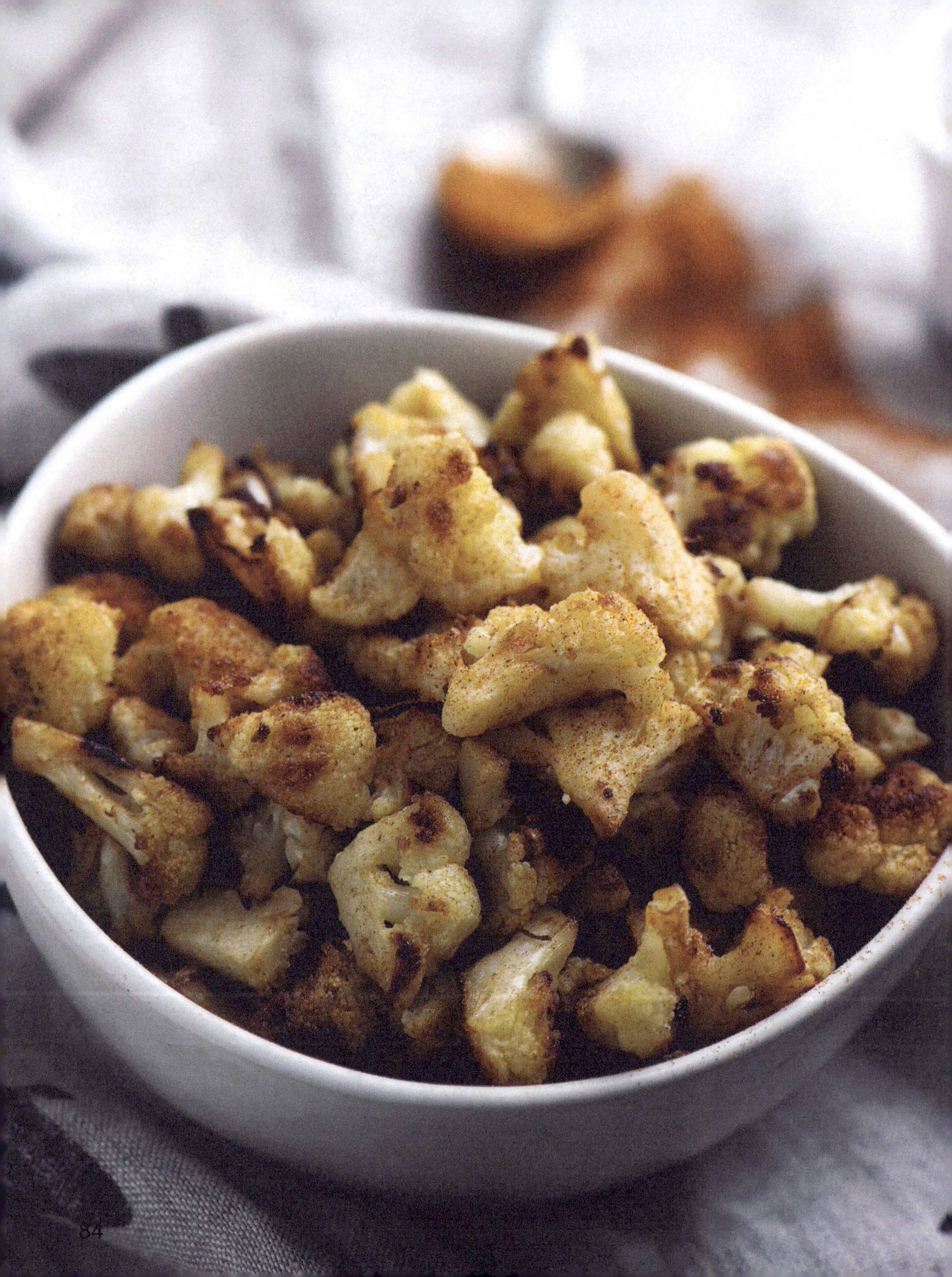

CAULIFLOWER POPCORN

| | Cooking Difficulty: 1/10 | | Cooking Time: 25 minutes | | Servings: 2 |

INGREDIENTS

- 2 cups cauliflower florets, bite-sized
- 1 tablespoon olive oil
- 1/2 teaspoon garlic powder
- 1/4 teaspoon smoked paprika
- 1/4 teaspoon turmeric
- black pepper, to taste

DESCRIPTION

STEP 1
Preheat the oven to 400°F (200°C) and line a baking sheet with parchment paper.

STEP 2
In a bowl, toss cauliflower with olive oil, garlic powder, smoked paprika, turmeric, and black pepper. Spread the cauliflower on the baking sheet and roast for 20-25 minutes, stirring halfway, until golden and crispy.

STEP 3
Serve warm as a crunchy snack.

NUTRITIONAL INFORMATION

90 Calories, 5g Fat, 8g Carbs, 2g Protein

86

RENAL-FRIENDLY PANNA COTTA

Cooking Difficulty: 2/10	Cooking Time: 25 minutes	Servings: 3

INGREDIENTS

for the panna cotta:
- 1/2 cup unsweetened almond milk
- 1/2 cup plain greek yogurt (unsweetened, low-sodium)
- 1 teaspoon unflavored gelatin powder
- 1 tablespoon honey or maple syrup (optional)
- 1/2 teaspoon vanilla extract

for the strawberry compote:
- 1/2 cup fresh strawberries, chopped
- 1 teaspoon honey (optional)
- 1 tablespoon water

DESCRIPTION

STEP 1
In a small saucepan, heat almond milk over low heat until warm (do not boil). Sprinkle the gelatin over the milk and stir until completely dissolved. Remove from heat. Whisk in Greek yogurt, honey (if using), and vanilla extract until smooth. Pour the mixture into two small serving cups or ramekins. Refrigerate for 2-3 hours, or until set.

STEP 2
In a small saucepan, combine strawberries, water, and honey (if using). Cook over medium heat, stirring occasionally, until the strawberries break down and the mixture thickens slightly (about 5-7 minutes). Let cool.

STEP 3
Once the panna cotta is set, spoon the cooled strawberry compote over the top. Serve immediately.

NUTRITIONAL INFORMATION

180 Calories, 8g Fat, 10g Carbs, 5g Protein

STRAWBERRY SMOOTHIE

| Cooking Difficulty: 1/10 | Cooking Time: 2 minutes | Servings: 1 |

INGREDIENTS

- 1/2 cup fresh or frozen strawberries
- 1/2 cup unsweetened almond milk
- 1 tablespoon plain greek yogurt (unsweetened, low-sodium)
- 1 teaspoon honey or maple syrup (optional)
- 3-4 ice cubes

DESCRIPTION

STEP 1
Combine all ingredients in a blender and blend until smooth. Add more water or plant-based milk if needed to reach desired consistency.

NUTRITIONAL INFORMATION

120 Calories, 3g Fat, 4g Carbs, 25g Protein

BERRY SMOOTHIE

| Cooking Difficulty: 1/10 | Cooking Time: 2 minutes | Servings: 1 |

INGREDIENTS

- 1/4 cup fresh or frozen blueberries
- 1/4 cup fresh or frozen raspberries
- 1/2 cup unsweetened almond milk
- 1 tablespoon plain greek yogurt (unsweetened, low-sodium)
- 1 teaspoon honey or maple syrup (optional)
- 3-4 ice cubes

DESCRIPTION

STEP 1
Combine all ingredients in a blender and blend until smooth. Add more water or plant-based milk if needed to reach desired consistency.

NUTRITIONAL INFORMATION

145 Calories, 4g Fat, 4g Carbs, 27g Protein

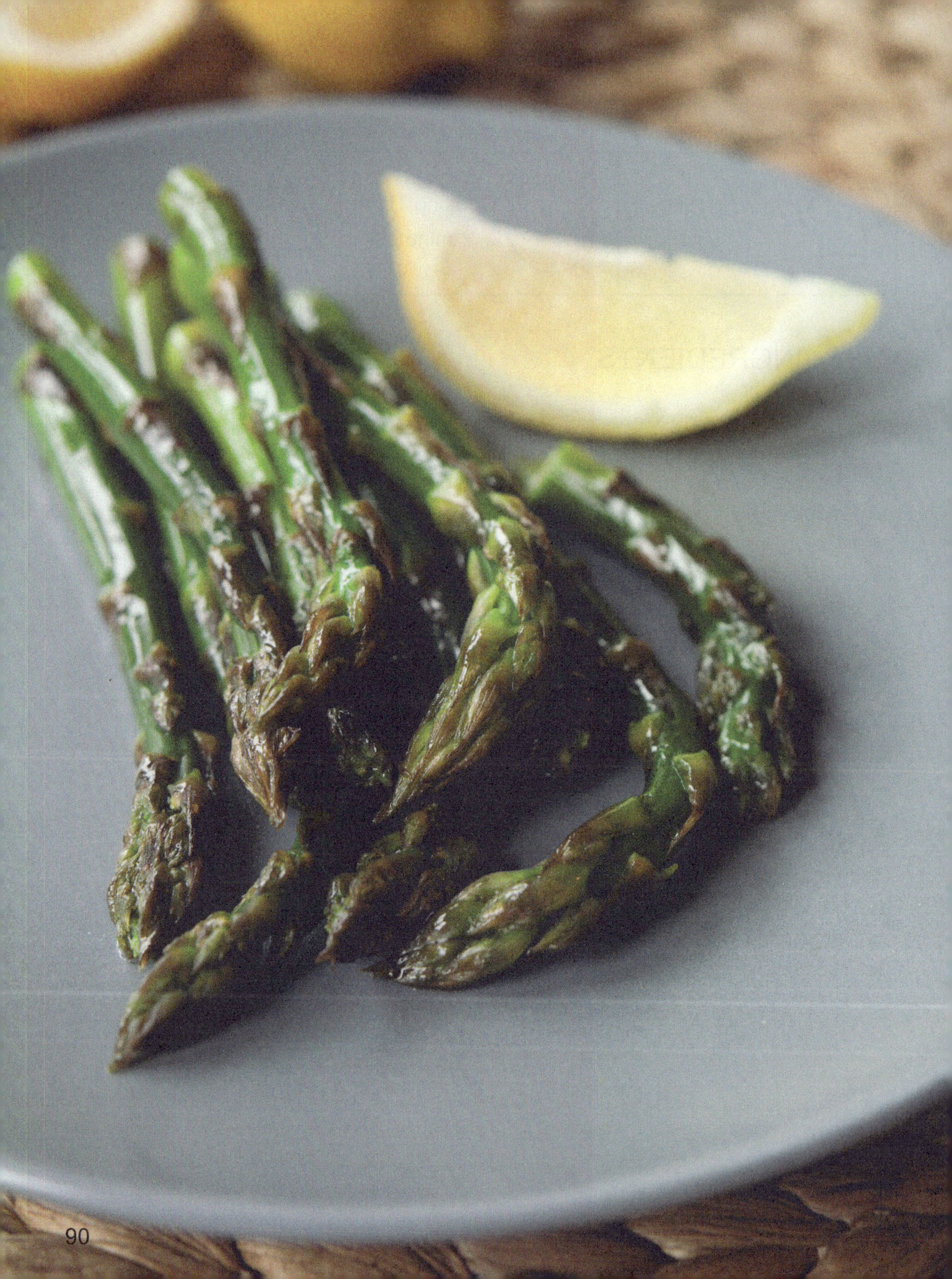

ASPARAGUS SPEARS

Cooking Difficulty: 2/10

Cooking Time: 11 minutes

Servings: 2

INGREDIENTS

- 1 bunch of asparagus (about 10-12 spears)
- 1 tablespoon olive oil
- pepper to taste (optional)
- fresh lemon juice (optional)
- fresh herbs for garnish (optional, e.g., parsley or thyme)

DESCRIPTION

STEP 1
Heat olive oil in a large skillet over medium heat. Add the asparagus spears and cook for 5-7 minutes, turning occasionally, until they are tender and slightly browned.

STEP 2
Remove from heat and season with pepper to taste (optional). Drizzle with fresh lemon juice and garnish with herbs if desired. Serve immediately.

NUTRITIONAL INFORMATION

70 Calories, 3g Fat, 9g Carbs, 4g Protein

CAULIFLOWER SPREAD

Cooking Difficulty: 1/10	Cooking Time: 7 minutes	Servings: 2

INGREDIENTS

- 2 cups cauliflower florets, steamed
- 1 tablespoon olive oil
- 1 tablespoon unsweetened vegan cream cheese low-sodium (optional)
- 1/2 teaspoon garlic powder
- 1/2 teaspoon dried thyme
- a squeeze of fresh lemon juice
- a pinch of black pepper

DESCRIPTION

STEP 1
Blend steamed cauliflower with olive oil, vegan cream cheese, garlic powder, thyme, lemon juice, and black pepper until smooth. Adjust seasoning to taste. Serve with fresh veggies or low-sodium crackers.

NUTRITIONAL INFORMATION

110 Calories, 6g Fat, 8g Carbs, 2g Protein

ZUCCHINI HERB SPREAD

| Cooking Difficulty: 1/10 | Cooking Time: 5 minutes | Servings: 2 |

INGREDIENTS

- 2 medium zucchini, chopped and steamed
- 1 tablespoon olive oil
- 2 tablespoons unsweetened plain vegan yogurt low-sodium (optional)
- 1/2 teaspoon dried basil
- 1/2 teaspoon dried oregano
- a pinch of black pepper
- fresh parsley for garnish

DESCRIPTION

STEP 1
Blend steamed zucchini with olive oil, vegan yogurt, basil, oregano, and black pepper until creamy. Garnish with fresh parsley. Serve as a spread or dip.

NUTRITIONAL INFORMATION

90 Calories, 5g Fat, 7g Carbs, 3g Protein

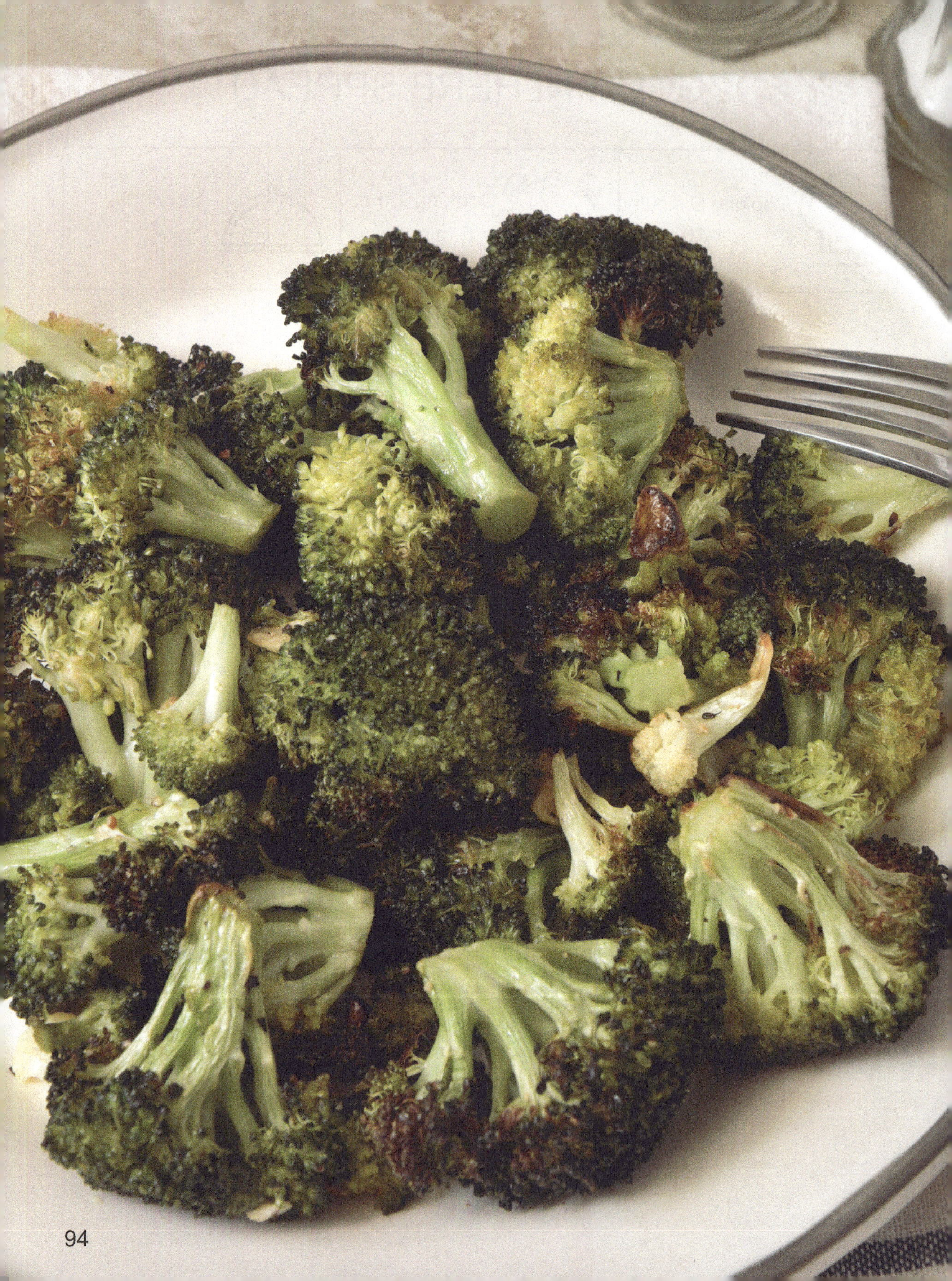

ROASTED BROCCOLI FLORETS

Cooking Difficulty: 2/10

Cooking Time: 25 minutes

Servings: 3

INGREDIENTS

- 2 cups broccoli florets
- 1 tablespoon olive oil
- 1/4 teaspoon black pepper
- 1/4 teaspoon paprika
- 1/4 teaspoon garlic powder
- pinch of red pepper flakes (optional)

DESCRIPTION

STEP 1
Preheat oven to 400 degrees F (200 degrees C). Line a baking sheet with parchment paper.

STEP 2
In a large bowl, toss broccoli florets with olive oil, pepper, paprika, garlic powder, and red pepper flakes (optional). Arrange broccoli florets in a single layer on the prepared baking sheet. Roast for 15-20 minutes, or until golden brown and tender.

NUTRITIONAL INFORMATION

100 Calories, 5g Fat, 10g Carbs, 3g Protein

CONCLUSION

As we age, prioritizing brain health becomes more vital than ever, and the MIND Diet offers a promising path to support cognitive function and overall well-being. Throughout this cookbook, we've explored not only the principles of the MIND Diet but also provided a wealth of delicious, nutrient-rich recipes designed to make healthy eating enjoyable and accessible.

By embracing the foods highlighted in this diet—such as leafy greens, berries, whole grains, and healthy fats—you can nourish your brain and reduce the risk of cognitive decline. The recipes included in this book are crafted with seniors in mind, focusing on flavors, ease of preparation, and nutritional benefits.

In addition to meal planning, we've emphasized the importance of adopting healthy lifestyle habits. From regular physical activity and mental engagement to fostering social connections, these practices work hand-in-hand with the MIND Diet to create a holistic approach to brain health.

Remember, every step you take towards healthier eating and living contributes to your cognitive vitality. Consult with your healthcare provider or a registered dietitian to tailor the MIND Diet to your individual needs, ensuring that you make choices that enhance both your brain health and quality of life.

By making the MIND Diet a central part of your daily routine, you empower yourself to embrace a vibrant and fulfilling life in your golden years. Let this cookbook inspire you to explore new flavors, enjoy nutritious meals, and prioritize your health—because your brain deserves the best care possible.

Samuel Hartwell

97